Wild Places
—— and ——
Gentle Breezes

JIM KLOBUCHAR

Wild Places
and
Gentle Breezes

Voyageur Press

Printed in Hong Kong
90 91 92 93 94 5 4 3 2 1

Library of Congress Cataloging-in-Publication Data

Klobuchar, Jim.
    Wild places and gentle breezes / Jim Klobuchar.
       p.   cm.
    ISBN 0-89658-143-8
    1. Outdoor recreation. 2. Newspapers—Sections, columns, etc. —
Sports 3. Minneapolis star and tribune. I. Title.
GV191.6.K57 1990
796.5—dc20   90—40143
                                       CIP

Published by Voyageur Press, Inc.
P.O. Box 338
123 North Second Street
Stillwater, MN 55082 U.S.A.
In Minn 612-430-2210
Toll-free 800-888-9653

Voyageur Press books are also available at discounts for quantities for educational, fundraising, premium, or sales-promotion use. For details contact the marketing manager. Please write or call for our free catalog of natural history publications.

In Jim Klobuchar's 25 years as a columnist for the *Star Tribune*, *Newspaper of the Twin Cities*, and the Minneapolis *Star*, he has taken his energies and his fondness for the far horizons to the Himalayas, the Alps, the American West, the Andes and Africa. With hundreds of thousands of readers he has shared his thrills, amusements, his encounters with the folk of those lands and his discoveries. In many of those places he has found himself spiritually enriched, and this, too, he has shared. He is a native of northern Minnesota, the author of ten previous books, a popular speaker and lecturer and the operator of a travel club, Jim Klobuchar's Adventure. In 1984 he was named outstanding general columnist among newspapers with circulations of over 10,000 by the American Society of Newspaper Columnists. He is one of the finalists among the candidates for space flight in NASA's Journalist-in-Space project.

Rod Wilson, who took most of the photographs that appear in this book, is an attorney living in Eden Prairie, Minnesota, and a long-time outdoor activist. His climbing ascents include peaks on four continents, and his other exertions have taken him to marathon runs and to winter wilderness areas of Yellowstone National Park and the Wind River Mountains. He and Jim Klobuchar have shared the climbing rope and the ski trail for more than ten years. As a member of the Minnesota Attorney General's staff for several years, he specialized in public utilities law, and today he maintains a private practice in Minneapolis.

CONTENTS

INTRODUCTION

Before I learned about the Seven Wonders of the World, I saw the cliffs and surf of Lake Superior. The scene seemed to me to be colossal, waters sweeping forever into the east and paved amber by the emerging sun. Could any ocean be bigger, any mountains grander than the precipices that shot hundreds of feet above the breakers?

In later years, I saw and climbed true mountains and crossed the oceans, roamed deserts and wildlife savannahs. None of those sights and sensations diminished the power of that first exposure to the vastness and the grace of nature. That was a special hour of conversion, because it kindled a wish that eventually became a sort of propulsion—to visit and to involve both body and the spirit in the faraway places.

This book is a journal of some of those episodes. It coincides with my 25th year as a columnist for what is now the *Star Tribune, Newspaper of the Twin Cities*. Much of this material appeared in the pages of the newspaper in a variety of forms, from travels commissioned in part by the newspaper. It is not quite correct to say they were "assigned." The editors took pains to disavow any liability for climbs in the Andes, solo camping trips in the frozen Boundary Waters in midwinter or bike rides across the wide Missouri. They took the position that a certain amount of irrationality is valuable in a columnist, as long as the contract harbors an escape clause. But they also assumed reasonable levels of prudence in what I planned, where I went and how I got there, and in my choice of companions.

I might have been more prudent in my choice of companions, but I couldn't have been more fortunate. There are no daredevils among them, and I certainly shun that classification. They are people who fill the range of temperaments, from the gentle mountain man of the west, Glenn Exum, to a restless goal seeker like Doug Kelley. I have lived for days with the comforting presence and introspections of Monte Later, and the sensible and modest competence of Rod Wilson, a lawyer-outdoorsman-photographer who took most of the pictures that appear in this book. John Peterson, the first and only man I've ever met who truly deserved the title of "ageless," practically forced me to reach the top of Devil's Tower. Kjell Bergh joined me in the 24-hour night of Spitzbergen and the Ngorongoro Crater of Africa. Amy Klobuchar shielded me from tedium on our bike rides by blowing a tire every other day. There were more, of course, including members of my very forgiving family, from Lois to my daughters.

These stories are not about people assaulting mountains and chasing the wind in the pursuit of raw thrill or notoriety. Going to the high country is in the glands of some of us, and there is no use denying it. So is riding cross-country on a bicycle, walking the trail to a woodland lake and feeling the west wind in the face. So is turning the corner of a trail for one more look into the forest. Most of us have urges like that. Many of the experiences chronicled here are nothing more than average people thrust into very uncommon parts of the world, enjoying those places or dealing with them.

In some of us the urges to feel and to exert in nature are more intense or more novel or, to be truthful, riskier. The commercial adventurer will often have to make cold-blooded calculations about risk, whether the outcome is worth the chance. The amateur adventurer makes those calculations only rarely, and not at all if he or she can avoid them. If there is serious risk, go back, change the route, try tomorrow or pack it in. Still, the accident will happen. In these pages is an account of one of those, and the pain of that experience is almost as strong today as it was the day a marvelous man died in the mountains.

My first adventure was walking in the woods with my father at the age of five in northern Minnesota in the early spring. I felt safe, and yet I will never forget feeling that I was also entering a world of mystery, sustained by some unlocked intelligence, where the woods were deeper than I had imagined and the snow higher than it ever got in the streets of my town of Ely. The mystery of the woods sent a soft charge through my body. A year later I saw Lake Superior, and the feeling returned. It is the same stirring I have felt the night before every climb, in the passenger seat of every plane carrying me to one more land, or perhaps the same land revisited one more time. The admonition that you can't go back again has never impressed me much. I go back to the Kali Gandaki trail in Nepal and Kilimanjaro in Tanzania, the Matterhorn in Switzerland and, since they're so tolerant, the cottage of Liv and Christian Bergh in Norway. There are friends to revisit, a time in your life to renew, places so good and memorable that seeing them again gives the searching life a more comfortable focus.

The majority of the photos in this book are Rod Wilson's. Others that require credit are identified. Rod shared some of the ventures with me, and from this armory of photos he was able to illustrate others. We couldn't bring back with us the climactic day on Huascaran in Peru. His camera jammed from the cold on the way to the summit. My film never was cranked on the sprockets, which is one more reason to be prudent in your choice of companions in the wild places. The rest of Rod's film was remarkable.

Some of the places you may have seen and may treasure from your own memories. If so, we are kin in a special way.

Jim Klobuchar
June, 1990

I.
North to Waterfalls and Wolf Calls

*Wild nature in parts of the world may herald its
mystique and celebrity. Northern Minnesota's
nature has something more durable—
an outdoors for all seasons,
all ages and most spirits.*

A BOY'S FIRST CAMPOUT IN THE WOODS

He wore a washed-out white sweater, embattled jeans and a pair of tennis shoes that had been through creeks and mudholes impartially.

He was a kid society calls fatherless, a 14-year-old boy from a broken family. His parents were divorced five years ago, and he lived with his mother in south Minneapolis. Until I met him at the Big Brothers' camp on Mille Lacs, we knew nothing about each other. At the invitation of a camp counselor, I found him at the camp's basketball court. He was methodically setting the camp record for missing the backboard on consecutive shots from 10 feet.

But Jimmy was fully geared for weekend adventure, it's destination unknown. It depended on the volunteer's name he drew from the camp's activity lottery. After we shook hands he put down the basketball and collected his expedition-and-survival gear for all occasions. In one hand he held a sleeping bag that might have belonged to Rip Van Winkle. In the other was a fishing rod, a tackle box and a small utility bag. The bag harbored a change of socks and underwear, a comb and a half bag of Planter's Peanuts. With this armament, Jimmy declared himself ready for the northern Minnesota wildwood and all foreseeable emergencies.

Somebody had told him about my suggestion of Lake

Superior's North Shore and Minnesota's Arrowhead country as a reasonable objective for two explorers. He wasn't a dynamic kid by nature. We both understood that a certain feeling-out process was necessary in these things. It couldn't be avoided by any surface cordiality. He was a kid who was alert and interested, a little cautious but also inquisitive. He had never been north of farms near the Twin Cities. He had never seen the big woods or camped under the stars. He had large round eyes and a head of brown hair that spread over his forehead in bangs and was usually left bare to the rain, sun or bush burrs.

"I'm a better fisherman than a basketball player," he confessed as we rolled along the shore of Mille Lacs and headed toward Duluth. Impressed, I thought it a good time to bare my own inadequacies.

"As a fisherman," I said, "I couldn't get a bite in an aquarium. I don't have a rod. Maybe you can show me some techniques. We may not find fish, but I think you may see something you haven't expected. We're going to see an ocean, right here in the middle of the country."

I described Lake Superior and handed Jimmy a map. He was the designated expedition navigator in charge of road signs and junctions. In less than two hours we had reached the cascades of the St. Louis River in Jay Cooke State Park and crossed the Interstate Bridge between Duluth and Superior, Wisconsin. Although it was late May, the ice pack of Lake Superior glistened to the northeast, as though signalling our arrival on another planet. Duluth weather has a deserved reputation for the bizarre, but this one came right out of the believe-it-or-not almanacs. The temperature a few miles to the west was 85 degrees. In Duluth, refrigerated by an ice field stretching 10 miles across, it was 25 degrees cooler— as if you woke up to find an iceberg in the middle of your front yard. But the water opened beyond Two Harbors 25 miles up the lakeshore and the sun touched its pale blue surface with streaks of silver. And now something almost as bizarre happened. Cautious and quiet Jimmy was jabbering like a jay, describing the freighter five miles out in the lake, twisting around to watch the gulls overhead and then staring down at the swell rolling against the shoreline.

"You're right. It IS an ocean," he said.

The irresistible place names declared the history and a little bit of the poetry of the North Shore as we drove—Castle Danger, Split Rock Lighthouse, Gooseberry Falls, where we lunched, Baptism River, Father Baraga's Cross. We detoured six miles up the old Toonerville highway from Ilgen City toward Ely, just to see the lake in its spreading immensity as we crossed the headland ridge 600 feet above it. And then we drove up the Sawbill Trail and picked a place deep in the woods with a small opening in the trees. Through it we could see the flouncing river below. We put up our orange and green tent and I went for water. When I got back, the kid had built a fireplace of boulders, dragged in firewood for a three-week retreat and seemed poised to light a match.

We discussed that. I said I thought a fire was one option, but since it was 4:00 P.M., some trail time before supper was another. He agreed, and we found trails. One was a trail to Eagle Mountain, where we hiked to the top of Minnesota's highest hill. He walked with energy and widening eyes and with a walking stick that he kept breaking and replacing. Several times I heard him running to catch up, and I found out why when I stopped at a bend in the trail. He would stop to listen to a woodpecker, or to examine the dead leaves of the forest humus. They weren't new to him. But their place in the forest, and his place in that forest, might have aroused new thoughts and wonder in the mind of a fatherless kid who had never walked the northwoods. At the top of Eagle Mountain a sign announced we were at 2,301 feet. Jimmy flopped on the handiest flat rock. But after a few minutes he stood and walked a few feet to glimpse the distant wilderness lakes sunk deep in the twilight.

He looked up and seemed to be working out his thoughts.

17

"What are you thinking?"

"I think that's great," he said.

"So do I."

We ate stew and meat loaf cooked on our small camp stove. And then we sat by the campfire and talked about what he was going to be, a carpenter, farmer or maybe a painter. He said he liked drawing pictures and he would draw some of the North Shore in school. Before we got into our sleeping bags, the moon eased out of the clouds and rode above the noisy whitewater of the Temperance River and we watched its progress for a while. The fire was still crackling. The woods were full of sound, from the river, the fire and the insects. The night was alive and amiable, and it was a good time for conversation. We talked about little things. I asked what he had done with his last walking stick.

"I left it against a tree on the end of the trail," he said, "case somebody needs it."

I doubt that the northwoods taught Jimmy that simple courtesy. It was something he brought to the woods, and it was a lovely gift. The next morning when I left at sunrise to walk to the river, he was balled up in his sleeping bag. Only a trace of early-morning dampness touched the bushes and young leaves of the birches. It hadn't rained lately. There was a suggestion of dust scent in the air. But it was overmatched by the musky sweetness of the humus and the smell of the spring-cleansed pines. I walked to the edge of the river. It was noisy and fast, sluicing around the boulders which were its natural defenses against intruding canoers. The sun was doing its morning dance on the river but nothing moved in the forest except for the leaf of an overhanging hazel bush. It got splashed now and then by the tiny geysers of water thrown up where the river scurried into the rocks near shore.

One other thing moved. Jimmy was at my elbow, carrying a fishing rod and big expectations.

"Do you think I could catch a trout in this river?"

"I'll put it this way," I said. "Do you want me to hold breakfast

18

until you catch a trout or should I set up a Plan B, the way they do it in the Pentagon."

"Do you mean should you boil some water and make that oatmeal in case I don't catch a fish."

I told him I couldn't have said it better. The earnest young provider studied the river and made a decision:

"Why don't you warm up the oatmeal while I go fish?"

I thought this represented a compromise that two reasonable people could live with. I walked back to the fireplace and left the boy with the river. The oatmeal was about ready when the fisherman returned with the verdict that no more trout lived in the Temperance River. I nodded and said his findings confirmed something I had suspected for a long time.

Right about there Jimmy decided it was time for a long howling laugh. The oatmeal was ready and excellent.

We struck the tent and cleaned up our camp. He was a fatherless boy, but somebody, undoubtedly his mother, had spent good and important time with him. He was polite and thoughtful and knew about dealing respectfully with nature. He separated the charred wood pieces methodically and piled dirt on them. He put some waste paper into his little utility bag and then, while I was bagging the tent, he walked a few feet into the clearing to be alone with the stream and the morning sun in the woods.

"Isn't it pretty?" he said.

I said it was.

"What I like best," he said, "when you come here by yourself like we did, it makes you feel that this belongs to you. I mean not for good. But just for now. Isn't it crazy that some people would come in here and make a mess and not appreciate how good this is? I want to come here again some day, and I hope it's just as beautiful."

I agreed. I told Jimmy that the professors who know about the environment call that "stewardship."

But Jimmy said it better.

Ambushed on the Kekekabic Trail

There are differences between being lost on the Kekekabic Trail in northeastern Minnesota and being lost in the Arabian desert. One of them is defined by the birds of prey that shadow the groping wanderer.

In the desert the hovering vigilantes may be a brood of vultures. Along the Kekekabic Trail, the same mission and potentially the same results are achieved by armadas of deer flies and mosquitoes. There are stories that people who have tried both the desert and the Kekekabic will take their chances with the desert and the vultures.

Three of us—Bob Leiviska, an insurance man from Golden Valley, Minnesota, and his teenage son were the others—had no such choice. Our situation was deteriorating. We were lost somewhere in the birch and jack pine jungle ten miles west of the Gunflint Trail. We still had 30 of the 40-mile route to cover, and only 24 hours to make a rendezvous with a previously arranged ride back to Duluth.

To add to the mounting grimness, we were running low on Off.

In a conference under a hazelnut bush late in the day, waving branches at the predators, I sorted out our options.

"Unless we pick up the Kek trail again somewhere along the

sloughs," I said, "we'll just have to camp here overnight and go back to the trailhead tomorrow. This would publicly brand us as greenhorns and bunglers.

"On the other hand, we can keep scrambling in search of the trail. If we find it, we can derive great personal satisfaction out of reaching a goal. The goal on the western end of this mess is Lake One, 30 miles away through brush, beaver dams, bogs, deer flies and mosquitoes."

The elder Leiviska weighed the options thoughtfully. "I think we should keep looking for the trail," he said, "for at least five minutes more."

As destiny would have it, we located the trail, snatching renewed misery from the jaws of escape.

Our objective before nightfall was to reach an abandoned lookout tower halfway down the trail. The term trail is offered generously. The Kekekabic was cut into the northeast Minnesota wilderness of the Superior National Forest in the 1930s as a fire trail and a work project for the Civilian Conservation Corps, a government youth project of the Depression days. It was never intended for recreational hiking. Much of it is overgrown and disappears into spongy muck or thicket. Although it has been blazed off and on by the federal government, it is not consistently maintained nor advertised. The forest service does not encourage hikers in the summer and practically strangles them if they ask for a permit in winter. People have died on the Kek in both seasons, from hypothermia in the winter and possibly from the ravages of loneliness in the summer, although it could have been from loss of blood to the mosquitoes. I spent my boyhood in the town of Ely, not far from the western end of the Kek Trail, and could recall none of the town elders ever taking seriously the thought of walking it for recreation. They saw the terrain as dense, bug-infested woods. No surveyor has called them inaccurate.

None of this means that the Kek in summer, in selected summers, can't be enjoyable and absorbing in part. It gives the hiker access to country that is as close to pure wilderness as any in the northwoods. You can encounter a partridge lounging heedlessly in a birch branch an arm's length away, and welcome the quiet sheen of a small lake beside the trail. There is a solemnity about it in the deepest woods. You will find a distant ridge of birches enticing. The noises are almost constant. But you have to concentrate to distinguish them, the singing birds, drilling woodpeckers, crickets, frogs and, of course, the mosquitoes.

I organized the venture in response to an editor who was probably trying to mooch a good story: Columnist Reported Missing in Uncharted Wilderness. He handed me a letter from a hiker who wrote a trail report:

"From the Gunflint entrance to Howard Lake eight miles away it is generally good, some spots obscure as to marking, mucky in spots, uncleared in spots, but not too bad. . . .

"Howard Lake to Kekekabic Lake. A jungle. Totally uncleared. Trail generally unmarked.

"Kekekabic Lake to Lake One. Approximately 2 miles after Hatchet Lake is a marsh one-quarter mile across, waist-deep, with no detour in sight. Dangerous for the inexperienced. The last two and one-half miles of the trail, from Snowbank Lake to Lake One, is a swamp. It took me two and one-half hours to negotiate it. Timewise it's not a bad trail. Three days to Kek Lake, one day from Kek Lake to Lake One. In general the trail can be successfully negotiated by anyone with at least one year's experience in Vietnam, carrying machete and wash and dry underwear."

I told the editor this was not a trail, it was a penance. I also told him that because of the lateness of the week and time constraints on the other side, we actually had less than two days to hike it. He grumbled at that and said: "What do you want, a golf cart?"

So I packed and called Leiviska. I did this not only because he was a fellow lodge member in the fraternity of the Iron Rangers of Minnesota—a group of people of mixed blood lines with much energy and occasional paranoia—I also did it because he and his son, Bob Jr., are reliable types and finally because they are Finns. Finns are renowned for their meditative silence. I thought this would be helpful on the Kek trail.

So now after our consultation and the decision to plod on, we planned to bivouac at nightfall and tell fireside stories between nabs of Leiviska's sirloin steaks. I warned him about those steaks. I said we ought to travel with light food that we could heat on the camp stove. Leiviska has lumberjack appetites and feared the threat of starvation during our two days on the trail. The other objection I had to the steaks was that Leiviska had slipped them into my pack during the distribution of loads. They were dragging the pack down and launching rivulets of juice around the jelly beans and into my rolled sleeping bag.

For an hour and a half the trail went agreeably. We had a floor of humus and were shaded by thick oak and maple. But as the sun neared the horizon the trail vanished in the brush. The tree blazes were tougher to read and the only distinct trail signs were the tangerine ribbons the forest service had tied to a branch here and there.

At 8:00 P.M. we decided the Kekekabic lookout tower seven miles away was out of reach and we reset the evening's goal for a trail junction a couple of miles to the west.

At 9:00 P.M. we decided the trail junction was out of reach and reset our goal for a lakeshore short of the junction.

At 9:30 P.M. we said to hell with the lake and unloaded our packs on a rocky knoll overlooking a stand of swamp spruce.

We had been slogging for nine hours, interrupting only for a 20-minute lunch stop and five minutes for the jelly beans. According to the maps, we had come no farther than 15 miles. This took us to the brink of tears, because it meant we had nearly 25 miles to cover the next day, even with a pre-dawn start, and only a quarter of a can of Off to cover us.

I offered to cook the sirloin. But Leiviska was game. He said forget it and we should settle for a can of pears. He then dug into

24

his pack and showed me the contraband—a mosquito juice he hadn't revealed. The boy, he said, had his own small bottle and could handle the world. The older ones, he said, had to look after themselves. "I've been saving this can of 6-12," he said. "They say it's faster than Off if it's calm out."

I grabbed the 6-12 and I was pretty greedy about it, like a sinking man reaching for reeds. Having greased up, we ate the pears and got into our sleeping backs. It was actually a lovely night. The air was motionless and smelled of pine, and the stars were floodlights.

But the night was alive with buzzing sounds. They came without mercy or fear. I have lived through mosquito assaults in bush, swamp, mountains and prairie, but I had never faced this kind of barbaric persecution. Sooner or later the sleeping bag had to be opened for breath, and it was the same as opening the seacocks to the sea.

"We should build a fire," I told Leiviska.

He said the smoke might bring bears.

"Why not get out the Off?"

He said he just threw away the empty can.

"Why not get out the 6-12?"

He said he was saving the rest of it for the kid, his own flesh and blood.

I thought an alternative might be to coat our skins with white gas from the cooking stove.

He thought we might explode if we tried that.

So we spent the night slashing and cursing the unseen assailants. Neither of us slept. The boy evidently had long since made his peace with the mosquitoes and drowsed happily, although well punctured. At 4:00 A.M. we got up and pitched into the murky wilderness by flashlight. We got to the end 16 hours later, 10 pounds lighter each and in mounting need of transfusions.

It was, in other words, the kind of northwoods idyll you dream about.

SUPERIOR'S SPEARS OF ICE

Rand-McNally does not classify Lake Superior's North Shore as therapy. It is geography, wind-blown water and ancient rocks. It is not supposed to be a prescription.

Yet judges and psychologists should seriously consider assigning those in their charge to a December day on the North Shore.

They could call it a therapy that makes no demands. Battling spouses should consider it for each other. Road builders should consider it for the thousands of motorists they disorient or lose in the craters.

On this day I had business in Grand Marais, Minnesota, which may be the surest rebuttal to the atheist's claim that God is dead. You don't get many reasons to travel to Grand Marais in winter unless you have providential help. But on the chance that you may be plotting the same somewhere down the road, or have your own North Shore in another part of the world, let me offer my day's travel journal. It's not the only way to experience a North Shore on an early winter day. But it's a way I know and enjoy.

You can clear Duluth by daybreak with an early start. It's a comfortable run from there to Two Harbors, and beyond there let the mind conjure the phantoms of Voyageurs, the singing little Frenchmen who may have given rise to the exotic place names of the lonely road signs—Castle Danger, Madonna of the Ice, and more.

Gooseberry Falls, the road map announces. The parking lot is deserted. Descend the snow staircase and confront the soundless cataract. No, it is not quite silent. The stream glugs faintly from somewhere inside the thickening ice imprisoning it. If you're careful you can walk the ice above the great white spears. Imagine. Walking the brink of a frozen waterfall, descending its buttresses and standing among the icicles, listening for the moving water?

A hundred feet below, the water works itself free, struggling for a brief liberation before the harder freeze of January. It sends amber spray onto the soft snow above its channel, creating a natural sludge that tomorrow will be ice.

It is the laboratory of the northwoods winter, working its austere chemistry.

But you don't have to adopt its moods. You may romp around here to wake up the woods. If you want to frolic, skim down the frozen stream bed for a while, skating among the balsams. You want to be careful, but you don't want to be timid, because how many times are you going to skate under a waterfall?

The sea beyond seems to shift character with its colors. It moves from lime to turquoise, gray to blue. The sun itself seems intimidated by the water's mood and can't decide how to confront it.

Lake Superior may be beautiful at certain hours and in certain dispositions. Yet even becalmed, it is not a sociable sea. The cascading streams keep it appeased in its better moods, but in its most natural attitudes it broods and it ponders and sometimes it fumes and then it seems to lie in contrition.

Not all oceans have to enchant. Not all of them have the gift for it.

There are no cars in the Temperance River lookout parking lot. Walk beneath the brilliant red berries of the mountain ash. They form a corridor above the trail to the cauldrons a quarter of a mile away, where the cascades hurl themselves into the rock amphitheaters, forming cliffs of ice and grottoes filled with foam.

The sun is fading as you leave Grand Marais and head for lodgings in Tofte. But it spills its dwindling light onto the restless sea, glazing it with silver. And a few hours later the east wind comes. It roils the sea, sends it crashing and screaming against the ancient rocks, until it seems almost to pound at your window. The breakers rise as the night deepens. It is a night without moon or stars, as though the heavens had yielded to the sea.

The sound of the freezing surf fills the room. The night is impenetrable to the onlooker, except for the rhythmic white crest of the breakers.

It's not a bad way to spend a night, if you aren't neurotic about needing quiet in your life.

A CHORALE OF WOLVES AT MIDNIGHT

The concert began 10 minutes before midnight. Its virtuoso soloist was the leader of the pack, piercing the motionless air with a howl that drifted from the ice of East Bearskin Lake into the crowns of the high Norway pines miles away.

There is no sound that so starkly defines the winter wilderness as a wolf baying in the night. For any human intruder within earshot, it stifles the breath and grabs the skin. It evokes a tormented loneliness and a sense of menace too vivid to be appeased by the calmer wisdom of the woods, that wolves have no history of molesting man.

A man lodging alone in a tent beside the frozen lake may understand the lore and find it reassuring, although not wholly convincing. They must have been a quarter mile away or so when the head vocalist and the rest of his chorale began. At that distance, I did not find the performance disagreeable. Only the leader howled during this movement; the others barked and yapped. It must be a sight. Imagine. A wolf pack in congregation under an almost full moon and flaming starlight on a February night in Minnesota's Boundary Waters Canoe Area.

I struggled out of my double sleeping bag, unzipped the front panel of the tent and looked out on the ice to the east.

They were in shadow in a bay, but their forms were visible, five or six, moving here and there. There was another howl, more yapping and snuffling. The temperature must have been 15 to 20 below zero, heading for 25 below. No thermometer was necessary. The suddenness of the pain in the fingertips, touching cold nylon and metal, was an accurate substitute for mercury. So was the instantly stiff hair in the nostrils and the stunning light show of the northern sky pouring down on the soft white velvet of the lake's snow cover.

The wolves stopped. Nothing moved or sounded over the great sweep of the imprisoned lake and the forests beyond.

Good-bye wolves. For a moment there, I suspected the erudition of the scientific wolf-watchers, who believe that the nocturnal wailing isn't wailing at all, but rather a declaration of joy by the pack. Togetherness. A family sing-along. Not a hostile note in it, the wise ones insist.

I apologized to the scientists for being momentarily deceived. So doing, I zipped back in and dozed for 15 minutes. Roll over now because a rib of snow under the tent floor has formed an uncompromising neck-to-kneebone ridge of ice that can't be ignored and has to be outwitted. Doze a few minutes more.

Another wolf howl, this one filling the tent with its unearthly siren, from a distance of no more than a hundred yards.

Jesus.

They were in my front yard, just off the shoreline from where I was camped in a grove of cedars. The barking seemed more urgent. That might have been the power of suggestion but there was nothing imaginary about the decibel count. It was running off the scale.

Wolves' admirers maintain there has never been a documented case of a wolf attacking man in northern Minnesota. As one of the admirers, I've never challenged the premise.

At this moment, however, I thought the record just might be incomplete. Maybe a few undocumented cases?

I tugged out of my downy cocoon again and trained a flashlight on my available armory: a Swiss army knife and four
aluminum minipots from my cooking set. If it came to battle, I was
going to defend myself by rattling four aluminum pots.

The prospect, if they were aware of it, did not appear to terrify
my visitors outside. The yelping accelerated. Were they simply
inquisitive? Were they sociable? How long had they gone without
a square meal?

I don't think I'll ever know. Trying to unzip the front door of
the tent again, I set off a racket that must have scattered the wolves
either in fright or bafflement, because when I looked out on the
lake again, it was flooded with innocent moonlight and nothing
more.

Something cracked in the woods behind me. It captured my
undivided attention, but it was no creature, that. The subzero air
was the performer this time, playing its percussions with the saps
and knots.

I was left to the night and its soundless musings. I slept,
occasionally.

I would have slept more in the Boundary Waters in summer,
when it is the settled habitat of the recreational canoeist and the
loon-seeker. Traveling alone in winter takes a different kind of
orientation of the mind and adjustment for the flesh. By most of
the values of touring and wayfaring, it is an unnatural act. It might
impose some risk and it certainly will present some discomfort.

One part of the wilderness experience is its pageant of exotic
sights and sounds, its remoteness and purities, and therefore its
grace and beauty. The other is the chemistry it creates within the
traveler. The experience can be vast geographically and powerful,
but it is not truly wild nature unless it bestows on the traveler one
of its deepest gifts—which is the intimacy and the kinship one
feels in its presence.

On a winter's day, or night, it may be harsh or lovely, convivi-
al or wrenching. But it is wild. And this adds another dimension.

In the 20th century, we live in unbroken interdependence. Every day, we see hundreds or thousands of people, hear hundreds or thousands of voices. But what if, every three or four years or so—and say you had the inclination, equipment, time and possibly the required fleeting spark of irrationality—you could spend 24 to 48 hours without seeing another person, hearing another voice?

Would it be worth the quizzical eyebrows of your friends?

Why, yes, assuming you were discreet enough to avoid the open water and to resist the impulse to schuss down a portage slope.

The risk in skiing and snowshoeing the frozen lakes and their portages for three days is marginal if the traveler is equipped and reasonably seasoned.

The time I skied onto Bearskin's lanky east-west lake, a trailing wind energetically shoved me over the hard pack. It was almost like sailing. I dug a pole into the scrabble and glided with a stroke, leaving me awkwardly unbalanced until I quickly leaned on the other ski. Once a quartering breeze did catch my backpack and almost flipped me.

The world's stubbiest spinnaker.

Poles and skis usually make creaking, squalling sounds slicing through the snow. The snow cover of East Bearskin was so hard it produced grinding, hollow noises of rapidly rising timbres as my body pressures shifted, like water filling up an empty jar.

If you ski cross-country, those sensations stick, because they are your companions for hours.

The thin crescent of Alder Lake's eastern arm broadened into the main basin, familiar to hundreds of summer canoers and campers.

For a day or two, in winter, it belonged to just one.

It is a heady idea, if not totally accurate. As visitors we come not as a proprietors but as witnesses. And while we may experience a quiet exultation being alone in the forest and coursing the lakes, we can never be totally at ease in this place in winter.

If it storms, we should be ready. There is a time for gawking and investigation, but when traveling alone in winter, one moves under constant imperatives that approach the force of religious codes.

Do not squander body warmth, and stay dry.

So I would put my camp in midday on the site of a summer campground beside the portage between Alder and Canoe lakes.

I raised my two-man Timberline tent 25 or 30 yards away, rested inside for half an hour, aired the sleeping bags in the crotches of a couple of pine trees and then skied uncluttered for two hours into little Pierz Lake to the east.

Some old moose tracks plodded through a bay there, and a weasel's precise little prints laced a small section near shore on the other side of the lake. Otherwise, it was barren of clues to wildlife. The probable truth was that there wasn't much around. You can call the winter animal life in the Boundary Waters wild, but you can't call it stupid. Much of what there is stays close to civilization, the few resorts open the year round, private homes whose owners make occasional visits in the winter.

Should the traveler be disappointed?

Hardly. The wolves can fill the void adequately at midnight.

A solitary glimpse into the northwoods, even only three days of it, tantalizes the intruder with games and mind pictures. I snowshoed on some of my explorations, plodding deep into the woods where no other human is likely to have come this winter. I had a rough destination, but mostly it was a pleasure cruise. Wind whooshed through the pines with those shifting surges and moods that give it an invisible personality. The temptation to imagine some kind of message in its sounds is irresistible. A welcome, a warning, a private hymn the traveler might detect but could not possibly interpret. That may be why the wind in the pines is so captivating. It seems to put the visitor on the verge of understanding, and it mingles its own yearnings with the human's. But it also beguiles and evades. Then it is silent, and the enigma remains.

Without company, showshoers conjure those fantasies, creating companions out of the trees in a way that gently mocks our search for solitude. If we lack the biologist's precise eye to identify all of the life and phenomena around us, we will often start looking at the woods allegorically. Sooner or later we all assign human values to the part of nature that is important to us. We do that out of fear, enjoyment or reverence. The sun is healing or the thunderclouds are malevolent. The wind is saucy. It is a harmless mental exercise that reminds us how desperately at times we want to immerse ourselves in the magic of wild nature.

So if there is nothing wrong with fantasy in the forest, what was it doing today?

It was full of pranks and teasings. An overhanging branch of a big black spruce forced me to scrunch as I passed underneath. I made the move flawlessly, without touching a twig. I straightened up in self- congratulatory attitude, and as I did, an unseen second branch lifted my cap clearly. Was that some kind of reprimand? Did I make a social blunder coming into this woodsy cathedral with my head covered?

Two yards farther on, a bough swatted me in the run.

And so it went.

I skied back into camp a few minutes after 5:00 P.M., spread the sleeping bags on a foam mat and aluminum-sheeted space blanket and lit the small cooking stove.

Now the chores. First to the creek, where the water rippled and chattered between great snow-duned logs. To reach it, I slid into the snowshoes and spraddled around until I was able to balance on two logs and dip my cooking pots into the water.

Don't fall here, baby. They might bring you back with a Zamboni from the Ice Center.

It was a fairly deft operation at that. Pleased, I maneuvered the big Alaskan snowshoes through the fallen timber and boulders, bearing the two water pots like an ungainly Gunga Din. Almost back onto the portage trail, I caught a hidden root with the tail of a snowshoe.

Both pots flew into the snow.

Back up the creek.

This time, I outflanked the root and arrived at my crude little kitchen with both pots brimming. In 10 minutes, I had boiling water and prepared now to answer the day's most provocative question: Can freeze-dried sausage patties be made edible by swashing them for five minutes in boiling water in their plastic baggies?

I emptied the water, as directed, and bit into the first of four sausage patties.

To put it modestly, the patties were marvelous.

At 5:45 P.M. I slid into my sleeping bag. The sun was dying beyond the pine crowns, and there was nothing to do but to outlast the night. I zipped to my nose and listened.

Every 10 minutes or so, something would crack, a tree vein in the below-zero air, my knee joint from the cramping, the ice far out on the lake, maybe something else.

At about the time I had it all figured, sleep crept up.

For 15 minutes. Then another crack.

The northland on a winter night is wild, and unforgettable, but not always poetic.

It is, however, almost always suspenseful.

II.
Walk With a Child's Eyes in Africa

Africa is lions and the nomadic Masai. It is jungle, desert, volcano and elephant grass, and a people in struggle. No one can see Africa in a week or in a lifetime. But what one sees fuses into the senses and will always be inseparable from them.

POISON ARROWS AND A REVEREND IN THE AFRICAN RIFT

A prismatic mist floated up from the dead lava cauldrons of the canyon floor 2,000 feet below the rim of the African Rift.

Was this real or some atmospheric trick, the river Styx lifted from mythology, a limbo of the mind?

Mount Oldonyo Lengai's volcanic cone rose spectrally out of the sulphur waves beyond the gorge. The walls of the equatorial pit shifted color from violet to lime to russet without logical explanation. Five miles away, the silver sheet of Lake Natron's soda basin reflected the volcano and the ages.

Somewhere beyond lay the Olduvai digs of the Leakey family, where the remains of humanity's forebears have been found. In the summer of 1988 we were walking past the probable cradle of the human race.

It was fitting that we had come here by foot. Another way to travel the rift valley is by Land Rover, an acceptably safe way to be thrilled by the animals and the convulsions of nature. But traveling wild Africa in the relative comfort of a Land Rover can create illusions. It can tempt the visitor to congratulate the world on how far it has come over the centuries. But moving on foot through African villages where sickness and ignorance kill will remind you that some of us and therefore all of us may not have come that far at all.

The six of us were walking 200 miles as a message to those of good will back in America that every dollar donated to meet an African need brings us closer to the ultimate kinship most of us profess.

A gun-packing reverend was at the head of our small entourage.

A couple of days earlier, near Loliondo not far from the Kenya border, Dave Simonson strapped on his Ruger .357 revolver and led us into a part of the valley where few white folk had walked before. In the darkness that morning we could barely distinguish the spreading umbrellas of the acacia trees under which we walked. The forest was not awake. A few hours before we had listened to the snuffling of hyenas outside our tents. Before nightfall, we watched astonished as a colony of nearly 60 giraffes strode over a knoll just beyond our campsite and into a grove of candelabra trees.

Not long after we began we heard lions bellowing to each other, 300 or 400 yards away.

We walked heavily after that, making sensible amounts of noise. You can do several things with lions in relative safety, but one thing you don't want to do is to surprise them.

East Africa might have been this way a thousand years ago, but today the reverend made it different. Dave Simonson wore a white beard and an Australian outback hat that conveyed the mixed image of Ernest Hemingway and Crocodile Dundee. He had wide shoulders and a bountiful gut and he waddled a little when he walked. Yet he strode powerfully and energetically for an overweight 58-year-old preacher, and he walked with uncommon good humor for a man leading us into a land of poison-arrow hunters.

"The Sonjo people," he said, "the arrow hunters, are friends of ours. So are the Masai. But the Masai are plains people. They don't go into the African Rift hills after the Sonjo cattle because they can't drive them over the escarpment without risking those poison arrows."

So we had nothing to worry about from poison arrows. These were people, after all, now conditioned to westerners—missionaries, traders, explorers, hunters and tourists. But the Sonjo don't find many tourists rubbernecking in the African Rift. The Rift is a 4,000-mile-long fissure in the earth's surface, nearly 30 miles wide, running from the Red Sea to the edge of the central African jungle. It was created by a vast volcanic power whose aftershocks are still evident in the eruptions of volcanoes we would pass in our eight-day walk. We were doing it not because of some special captivation for lava dust or poison arrows but because the reverend is a special kind of dreamer.

He is the kind of dreamer with the red clay of Tanzania under his nails and sweat in his armpits and a steady hand on the Ruger 357, but a dreamer still. He sees clinics and classrooms in the villages of the Masai and Sonjos and the others. He sees babies with something more in life than malaria and lung disease. When he came to Africa 30 years ago it was primarily to save souls as a Lutheran missionary. This objective was mildly applauded by the villagers whose souls were being saved. But Simonson discovered early that food, medicine and schools were just as urgent as heaven in the lives of most of them. So he and his wife, Eunice, a nurse, artist and an altogether remarkable human being, divided their energies equally toward those ends. They also found ways to stir the consciences and collection plate offerings of thousands in America. The result has been hundreds of schoolrooms and a handful of clinics that have brought health and perhaps the greater miracle of learning to thousands within their reach.

"What are you saying about the route today, Reverend," somebody asked.

"Today we have to worry only about snakes, leopards and tsetse flies. I've got the Ruger because you never know when you're going to surprise something and incur instant hostility. I'm talking lions and leopards."

43

It has been nearly 30 years since his first encounter with a lion. He came out of Concordia College and later the seminary with a yen for service in Africa, which was shared by his wife. They were still charged with idealism that first year when the elders of a Masai village, where they brought the gospel, asked Dave Simonson first about his rifle.

A lion had attacked the village twice, killing cattle and threatening the people. He would come a third time to kill humans, they were positive. They said their spears might not stop it, and they asked if he could help. They were serious and the reverend was scared. But he said he would. At dusk he parked his Land Rover outside the village. Shortly before sunset he heard the lion coming. Grunting and sniffing, it stopped and crouched, a blackmaned beast with an enormous head. Simonson dismounted. He heard the lion roar, and he trembled. Nothing in wild Africa is as terrifying as the roar of a lion when it is near. It engulfs the earth and bores into the recesses of the gut. Simonson dismounted. He had never fired the rifle, and never seen a lion that close. He held the rifle to his shoulder and fired. The lion fell dead. The young missionary was still shaking when the Masai villagers arrived with their shouts of thanksgiving. And the next day, there was an impressive new roster of Masai converts in church.

Nothing is more striking on a walk in the African savannah than the Masai, the herdsmen-warriors with their glistening skin and their imperial carriage. Westernization is reaching them slowly, but it will be decades before they abandon those spears and staffs and their nomadic dominions. On a knoll beyond a small ravine near our campsite, two Masai women braided their hair. They were tall and slender, wearing red wraparounds and trinkets in their hair that caught the sun and bound us for a moment of recognition and whimsy that bridges the cultures. I waved to them and they giggled and waved back.

They seemed content and not especially curious about their transient neighbors. Why should they be? We, too, would pass.

44

Just as drought, tribal wars, earthquakes, fires and a multitude of calamities in their history have passed. Television may be something else. It will get there eventually and already is creeping close. Wars have pretty much disappeared in the East African highlands, although there are still squabbles between Masai and Sonjo over cattle and water rights. The Masai's native religion, apart from conversion, is an absorbing mixture of traditional God-belief and devotion to nature and tribal convenience. It teaches, for example, that the Masai are the original and rightful owners of all cattle. This produces a pardonable objection from other tribes, who don't like the idea of the Masai asserting some doctrinal claim on somebody else's cattle. In the American West, most folks call that rustling. Simonson deals gingerly with these customs as well as with the social ones. He learned the languages long ago, delivers his sermons in those languages and trades bush gossip and advice in them.

"Some places," he said, "diplomacy breaks down and you just have to say 'no.' My sons and I visited a Masai village years ago and I had done something the elder was convinced was miraculous. He invited us to spend the night in his house, and I was the guest of honor. They passed around a gourd of milk. The gourd had been recently used to collect cow's urine, which the Masai sometimes use in cooking. The custom is that you drink all of what you are offered. I was first in line and passed on the concoction to my sons untouched. I told the boys as privately as I could: I don't care how you do it, just make sure that gourd is empty when it comes back to me.

"It came back empty, and I didn't ask any questions. The elder said he thought I was a great man and it would be an honor for him if I shared his bed with his wife and him. I said thanks a million but the bed isn't big enough for three of us because I'm too heavy. He said no problem, he would be glad to sleep in another bed. I've forgotten what my diplomatic language was, but it wasn't adequate and in the end I simply said I was so overwhelmed with humility in the face of the man's kindness that I just couldn't accept."

We descended more than a thousand feet into the gorge. In our party were the missionary, Donna Reed, a former librarian from Atlanta, Georgia, now committed to African causes; Dick Hefte, a Fergus Falls, Minnesota, lawyer; Mark Jacobson, an African bush doctor and director of a clinic at Arusha in Tanzania; Kjell Bergh, a businessman from Edina, Minnesota, the husband of a woman born in Tanzania and a partner with the Simonson family in the operation of a safari lodge; and myself. The African Rift is no Grand Canyon as spectacle nor constant Death Valley as an eroded wasteland. It was formed by cataclysmic explosions underground that split the continents and formed the Red Sea. Upheaval created a depression running from the Middle East to north of the Union of South Africa. Parts of it, in Ethiopia, are the cracked flats of a desert where nothing grows. Parts of it are fertile grazing ground and savannah for the wildlife. Some of it is forested. And here on the downslope toward the alkaline lake of Natron, it was capable of supporting cattle, but not well.

Outside a Masai village, we met Phillip. He stood six-foot-four, his black skin gleaming in parts not covered by his vermilion toga. He smiled confidently at us and held his long spear without showiness.

"Jambo habari," we said in greeting.

He nodded and replied in perfect English. "Welcome to our part of the world. And where, may I ask, are you going?"

He had been educated in Christian schools and an English university. But he was a Masai before he was anything else, and today he was tending his cattle, watching for lions and thieves. In his bearing, he might have been a Roman centurion. The comparison is not necessarily far fetched.

Simonson talked of one theory of the Masai origins. "Some of their weapons are close to what the Roman soldiers introduced in North Africa. There may be some trace of the Roman occupation in their genes. It's just a theory. It's extremely important to be respected within the Masai community. Losing that status can be a living death. Some northern Europeans offended a few of the Masai around here a few years ago. The Masai attacked them, killing two and wounding the others. It was homicidal, and it shouldn't have happened. The courts got involved and the justice decreed by the tribe was that the Masai would be ostracized. Nothing was ever heard from them again. They were exiled from their community, and to a Masai that is the brand of the living death."

We walked past the Masai village, past the little hut where four young people were loudly arguing over cups of homemade grog. Call it the cocktail hour in the African Rift.

It was late afternoon and the heat came seething up from the volcanic ash. We were walking beneath the flanks of Oldonyo Lengai, the volcano and the mountain of gods. We were just a few hundred yards from the soda flats and motionless water of Lake Natron, which might have been the Dead Sea. This was a lake out of a geological horror history. It was created by vulcanization and underground chemistry and gave off alien stenches. But just a few feet off shore there was a slash of brilliant pink, nearly a mile long. It was fragile but glorious, and it looked like a mirage until we recognized them. Flamingo by the thousands.

The heat seeped into our nostrils, our toes and our guts. It got into the cracks of the body and smothered the pores, and the misery that wasn't delivered by heat arrived with the dust.

Nobody complained much. We came to dramatize a need of thousands of kids who never read a schoolbook nor write a lesson under a roof. We had commitments that would make those buildings.

At day's end, the Masai in the village where we tented allowed us the use of the River of the Woods. We looked more mummy than human. The dust was that thick. In time we emerged from our convalescence after the usual 24 to 27 miles and were invited to bathe in the river. With chores to do first, I was the last to duck behind the thorn bushes to strip.

All right, I have seen movies like the African Queen. I know the scenes in the others where the unsuspecting bush novice jumps into the river for the luxury of a bath and meets the unattractive fate of becoming a crocodile's lunch. I jumped into the river. I brought soap and rising exhilaration. I bathed for nearly a half hour. The water was cool and swift and redemptive. It was so good it wouldn't have made one bean's difference if they warned me about lions and leopards in the nearby bush. They did, and it didn't make any difference.

Nobody said anything about crocodiles. I can't tell you right now whether there are crocodiles in the River of the Woods, and I really don't care to know. I do know that at the end of the plunge, I was clean in the African Rift.

It was a novelty.

And it didn't last long.

THE EXHAUSTED LIONS OF NGORONGORO

The lions were sunning themselves in attitudes of semi-exhaustion, postures that would never get them a screen test at MGM.

Driving down the switchbacks of the 1,800-foot slopes of the Ngorongoro Crater's green caldera prepares you for magnetic sights in one of the earth's great wildlife refuges, the home to more than 20,000 animals. But it did not prepare us for a love den of lions, all of them hopelessly groggy, lying in the grass, inviting the breeze. A hundred yards away, their natural prey, herds of zebras and wildebeests, grazed with impunity. A drowsy male lifted its massive head and rolled over onto his front paws as we approached. He regarded us with eyes intended to convey that classic leonine attitude of judgment and ferocity, the same one you have seen at curtain time of a thousand movies and on a hundred monuments.

He never quite made it. After holding the pose for a few seconds, he yawned and fell asleep on the neck of his adored. Before that, he gave his tail a labored swish that plainly declared his wishes to the intruders.

Go away, man.

Let me ask you a question. If you spend the whole weekend in the arms of amour, could you look ferocious with a hot sun beating on your back?

Be generous. Empathize.

Our Land Rover driver, Joel, a Masai who had attended college and was fluent in English, seemed to enjoy our amazement and did his best to choreograph it with a running banter on the mating habits of African wildlife. We came to spend the night in the Ngorongoro, a vast animal sanctuary, 12 miles across and so bountiful that it stirs inevitable comparisons with the Garden of Eden. The comparison may not be so wild. Humans may have begun not far from the Ngorongoro, if the Leakey's excavations in the Olduvai Gorge are credible evidence of that theory. To many researchers, they are.

Joel had emerged from the olive trees and orchids in the tangled forest growing on the rim of the crater. He was shorter than most Masai, wore western clothes, spoke English and carried a baptismal name that reflected his education in Christian mission schools. He revealed a frolicking personality that set us straight on the behavior of the lions.

"We happened to come in the middle of the mating season," he said at the campfire. "You can't believe how many times those lions get together in one day in the mating season. You saw they were so tired I could have run over them with the Land Rover."

It is the price of passion in equatorial Africa.

"Lions sometimes do it 50 times in one day," Joe said.

Aw, come on.

"Why do you think they call the lion the king of beasts? It's true. They barely have enough energy left to eat. Mating season is a great time to study the animals. Lions aren't the most interesting. The best are the ostriches. They sway. It's almost like a dance. Very graceful creatures. On the other side, there are the rhinos."

There undoubtedly are. There is almost nothing in the animal world that can't be found in the Ngorongoro, in its pastures and savannahs and luminous waters. In the middle of the crater is a fresh-water pool where hippos grunt and plop around and splash water on themselves. Flamingos mass on the soda lake nearby. Somewhere near the caves two miles away, a pair of spotted cheetahs wait for their hunger pangs to restart the stalking cycle. Wildebeests by the thousands honk on the plain. They are earnest but silly-looking beasts that might be God's revenge against the evolutionists. The wildebeest has the face of a skinny buffalo, the body of a horse and a grunt like a baritone kazoo. It is also called the gnu, and when you study it, you are tempted to ask, why not?

Emerging from the rock clump near the water are a black rhino and her baby. The rhinos are vanishing and almost helpless, the victims of poachers who kill for the horn. They are huge and clumsy and pitiable. There are fewer than 20 left in the Ngorongoro. The approaching extinction of this armor-plated dreadnought, so long a symbol of the prehistoric mystery and power of the jungle, is enough to bring tears.

Perhaps it can be saved. Africa is aroused about the deepening threat to elephants and rhinos posed by poaching. But whether it can sustain its new and highly publicized campaign to save the endangered animals may depend more on global arousal than on the thin resources and the resolve of African governments laced with internal corruption.

Yet if these homely rhinos only knew how many friends they have.

The amber light of late afternoon in the crater dissolved quickly into the descending night. The clouds gave way and a full moon rode above the fig trees that sheltered our tents. No other humans were here tonight. We slept in a campsite intended for the public, but all other travelers to the Ngorongoro slept tonight in the lodges above us on the crater rim. The sounds on the crater floor were incredible. A few feet above us, hyraxes—little animals that look like rabbits but are actually related to the elephant— screeched and yammered. Wildebeests honked and munched grass a few feet from our tent. Zebras snuffled and yipped around the tent entrance. And then shortly before midnight, the lions came.

They growled and grunted. I told Joel the mating season must have ended. Joel, sleeping amiably, didn't hear. The lions' grunting graduated into a roar, no farther than 50 yards from the tent. A half hour later, I was seized by the demands of nature.

Let me define a dilemma for you.

Here was this demand, and there were the lions.

I don't think I'm going to confide to you the solution I chose. You wouldn't want the jungle to surrender all of its mysteries.

III.
The Not Always Normal Norway

For a country of a few million people, Norway has had an extraordinary impact on the way people live and think in a substantial part of America. A visit to its mountain villages and fjords, and its long days and nights, might explain why.

GROPING THROUGH SPITSBERGEN'S POLAR NIGHT

Each year I put a star on my desk calendar's square for March 11, with a note: "Big party for the human penguins in Spitsbergen. Eat your heart out."

Sometime around March 11, a thin shaft of sunlight breaches the fortress of night on the earthen iceberg called Spitsbergen, an island the size of West Virginia a few hundred miles from the North Pole. Sometime during the day the sun will touch the steps of the old Lutheran Church after a five-month exile. A noisy feast is sure to erupt at that moment in a town called Longyearbyen, which by agreement of most cartologists and a few awed winter visitors lies at the literal end of the earth.

I have been one of those night visitors, and I will freely testify that I have never been so close to falling off the edge. I feel the tugs of envy to share that moment of solar redemption, because I spent a week there in midwinter, when the Big Dipper stood straight on its handle and blazed away in the black sky at high noon.

There are no actual penguins in Spitsbergen, of course. The

penguins live in Antarctica. Animate objects that live in Spitsbergen are called Norwegians. Polar bears, called ice bears by the Norwegians, also live there. About 25 miles from the Norwegians are Russians. Once a year the Norwegians and Russians get together to play games and to remind themselves how truly crazy this all is. The ice bears, probably agreeing, avoid them.

But on March 11, or thereabouts, the Norwegians celebrate their liberation from nearly a half year of round-the-clock night. It isn't your basic Mardi Gras bacchanalia with mob scenes and jazz bands. There is something about the Norwegian disposition that is not quite compatible with orgies on the glacier. What they do is to cook up pots of reindeer stew. With this and other Nordic tasties they put on a polar smorgasbord at the village canteen and sedately drain two weeks of the month's allotment of grog from the coal company store.

After that, a dozen of them may squeeze into wet suits, run down to the fjord, cast off among the ice floes and launch the training season for the northernmost windsurfing club in the world.

My eyes mist up at the thought of it. I hanker for the sight of those ice floes and arctic surfers, a spectacle I may never see. The only time I witnessed Spitsbergen was in January, which is not the month the national tourist office suggests. But I left reluctantly. It was one of the most flabbergasting weeks of my life, and it cannot possibly be duplicated anyplace else on earth that is reachable by commercial airplane, because nothing like it is.

The sky at noon is the color of crude oil. For directions you don't look down the street for road signs, you look overhead for Polaris. Silver mountains thrust into the blackness as though electrified. Ice stretches to the horizon, filling ravines and paving the tundra. Kids go to a school that is fenced against polar bears. Reindeer bound through the playground. A few miles away, miners burrow thousands of feet deep in the earth to dig coal that nobody needs. Down the coast the Russians are doing the same thing just to keep an economic foothold on the island, which is what the Norwegians are doing. Since the Norwegians grant commercial rights to scores of countries on Spitsbergen, anybody can do it. Because nobody buys it, nobody else mines coal there. Who would want to, except Russians and Norwegians? They don't quarrel with each other. They get along beautifully by ignoring each other.

Spitsbergen.

Spending a week on this island in winter, less than 700 miles from the North Pole, compares with conventional tourism in the same way as the flight to the moon compares with a balloon ride in shopping center.

Nothing prepares the visitor for winter in Spitsbergen, who is thrust into an ice-locked void, the psychological equivalent of weightlessness. It lasts from October to March, unrelieved by the faintest symptom of the sun, although by noon in February the sky does graduate to deep indigo. But the stars keep orbiting around the clock and around the world's most remote enclaves of civilization—the Norwegians' Longyearbyen and the Soviets' Barentsburg. Each supports close to a thousand souls, all of whom must by now have performed enough penance to earn bonus points for salvation.

My companion was Kjell Bergh, a Norwegian-born Minneapolis businessman who had proposed a recreational visit to Spitsbergen, which is the main island of an archipelago the Norwegians call Svalbard. Bergh had in mind a visit in July. I insisted on January as one possible way to discover the source of the Norwegian gift—seen often in Minnesota—for stoutly insisting on making sense out of the illogical.

Bergh examined that accusation. He said if I had this theory right, going to Spitsbergen in winter made me the honorary Norwegian to end them all.

We flew by SAS at night, of course. There are flights in and out once or twice a week. It was also cold and blowing a gale, of course. But an offshoot of the Gulf Stream moderates the temperatures enough so that the norms aren't really much different from Minnesota's. In fact, after the winds of our arrival, I often walked around bareheaded in temperatures that didn't fall much below five degrees Fahrenheit. Bergh and I had tinkered with a plan to spend at least one night in the open air in a tent, to get some notion of the arctic wilderness. The settlers considered this plan and responded with muted oaths of incredulity. They said nobody with a clear mind and a reasonable bias for a long life camps in winter in Spitsbergen.

"Even in summer," one of them said, "you can get a shock here if you try to sleep out. We had a TV team in here from Oslo a couple of years ago. They put some tents on a part of the tundra that looked good for a campground. Somebody must have had the same idea a hundred years ago, because one day a crewman saw something sticking out of the ground. In time he recognized it as a former camper. It was a skeleton, brought to the surface by the permafrost. They had camped on top of an old graveyard from the days of whaling and trapping. Nothing stays buried very long up here.

"Speaking of that, the location wasn't very far from where some Austrian researcher left his tent to try to run off a polar bear a year ago. The polar bear misunderstood his intentions and ate him."

Anxious to avoid any such communications breakdown, Bergh and I accepted accommodations in the coal company's guest quarters, where we sometimes were entertained by the art and wisdom of the island's poet laureate, a dentist named Leidulf Hafsmo, a Spitsbergen resident for years. Hafsmo is an authority on human defenses against isolation. It's hard to imagine a man better qualified, unless it might be the Prisoner of Zenda.

"There is no mass despondency in winter here," he said. "I think most of us find it quite agreeable. People assume we're lonely, but that's really not the word. Years ago, perhaps, when there was no air access and people were locked in by pack ice for six months of the year. People who come here now tend to deal well with things like privacy and a quiet, ordered life. Nothing much happens here today that didn't happen here yesterday. It was dark yesterday and it's going to be dark today. You will see the same people today you saw yesterday. Only the weather changes. It was cold yesterday and it may be colder or warmer tomorrow, although it could be the same."

Spitsbergen.

Spitsbergen is so far north that the Vikings, after discovering it in the 12th century, 500 miles north of the northern tip of Norway, shunned it for the next 300 years. Instead of trying to colonize it, they chose easier pursuits such as crossing the Atlantic.

Spitsbergen is so far north it is off the maps in some American schoolrooms. It is an eerie but gripping fluke of nature, a wind-wracked clump of ice mountains, tundra and glacier, but conversely a dramatically scenic place in the midnight sun. But in autumn when the sun sinks under the horizon for five months, the blackness becomes a fundamental condition of life in the same way that the desert heat dominates the Bedouin. It means that everybody who lives under its autocracy has to learn some psychological tricks to stay useful and socially agreeable.

Some of them practice a buoyant form of denial. Here was a school teacher of dazzling Viking structure and penetrating eyes, Anna Thorarinsdottin. She is a native of Iceland and a woman of broad comfort zones, because she insisted the long night gives her peace. "I think all of us need private times and thoughts in our lives. The Spitsbergen night is a cover for you. You can move as you wish. Nobody has to know where you are going or where you are coming from."

She smiled with a trace of enigma. Only the northern stars can tell you much more about Anna. If the night is mystery, Spitsbergen would have been paradise for Agatha Christie. But not every

Spitsbergener prizes secrets. In fact, very few can entertain them. Among the thousand or so dwellers in Longyearbyen, practically nobody was fooled by Lillian Saerter's tan. Lillian is a clerk in the little department store of the village's shopping district. She gave the appearance of a woman who just stepped off the plane from a four-month vacation in the Bahamas.

"I wasn't in the Bahamas," she said. "Ingeborg Mork did it. She runs a salon where you can take sunlamp treatments in a 10-step program. You can look like you've been lying on the beach in Florida all winter. Actually, I've never been south of Oslo."

Spitsbergen is no repository for the mavericks of Norwegian society. "Most people are here because they want to be," said Henrik Varming of the government-run coal company. "The miners can do well financially, but it's not the only reason they're here. This is big nature here. A lot of Norwegians like it that way, in the summer especially, when it's quite beautiful and comfortable. To make it in the long winter, you have to have a pretty stable personality. If you bring emotional problems or drinking problems here, they're going to be aggravated by the night and the isolation, and this would be a disaster for that kind of personality."

There may be slightly more drinking than Henrik acknowledges, but people who live in this darkened deep freeze do develop a fraternity and self-mocking amusement that surfaces in their entertainment. They party without excuses for it. They party when the sun comes out and when it disappears. They find holidays long forgotten on the mainland. A few years ago they were joined by an internationally known Norwegian singer who was booked for Paris but took the wrong plane and wound up in Spitsbergen. It was the all-time record for culture shock.

They never quite stop being Norwegian. The badge of membership in the middle-class lodge in Norway is to own a cabin up north to get away from the asphalt for a few days of solitude. The tradition persists, implausibly, on Spitsbergen. Scores of citizens in the town at the end of the earth own cottages 20 miles inland. "A person now and then has to get away from it," Varming explains.

He didn't explain what is it they're getting away from.

These cowsheds, more than a hundred years old, have resisted both the Alpine gales and the dictates of modern architecture.

A climber skirts a cornice while going for the top of the Eiger from the Mittelleggi Ridge above the north wall.

The great red cliffs rise hun-
reds of feet above the Lake
uperior North Shore at
alisade.

A canoeist far below the bluff reflects and may be about to check that compass.

Spreading its blue waters elegantly to the horizon, Ensign Lake is one of the gemstones of Minnesota's Boundary Waters.

Lake Superior's North Shore i marbled with rivers and waterfalls. Baptism Falls is one of the most memorable.

Hurtling through the woods
on its way to Lake Superior,
the Temperance River gets
ready for a fall–and a cavern.

Streamers of moonlight lace
the entrance of the Temperance River to the inland sea
that is Lake Superior.

Africa is boundless in its
power to engage the senses.
The sun sets over the acacias
in the Rift Valley of Tanzania.

The Rev. Dave Simonson saw
hundreds of needs in Africa,
stayed and became an institu-
tion.

Strolling in the sun above the Serengeti plain, four giraffes stand tall — since there really is no other way.

The arrow tip is full of poison but this time it's target practice.

A Masai herdsman glides
through the Tanzanian savannah.

Although poachers have killed elephants by the hundreds of thousands in Africa, this one seems secure in the marshes of the Ngorongoro.

Lions are ferocious when they have to be, and affectionate when it seems to be the right time. Mating season in the Ngorongoron Crater is one.

When the sun finally arrives in Spitsbergen, it's worth a prayer and a celebration.

When polar bears want to drift on an ice flow, the sensible thing is to let them drift.

Freighters, shrimp boats and yachts crowd the harbor of Bergen, whose residents claim their own culture, but share the fish.

Mosses, snows and the cold transparent waters of a mountain lake in Norway will cool the hiker's soles and leave a little sustenance for the soul.

Descending the renowned
Bessegen, the skyline trail in
Norway's Jotunheimen
Mountains, where, in legend,
Peer Gynt rode a reindeer.

The Devil's Tower in eastern Wyoming is a geological freak—but a dicey one for climbers like Doug Kelley (right) and Rod Wilson.

Wedged between pillars in the Devil's Tower, John Peterson probes for leverage.

Climbing above a broken column and into the crucial pitch of the ascent of Devil' Tower.

The Matterhorn flings its classic contours above the Arolla pines and wildflowers of the Zermatt valley.

Not far away, modern hotels and condos haul in tourists to the Alpine resorts, but the mountain hamlet of Zum See serenely ignores progress.

Behind Rod Wilson on the summit ridge of the Matterhorn is the iron cross installed decades ago on the Italian side.

SKIING WITH A NORWEGIAN FLYING LADY

Her hair was the texture of fluffed wheat. Her eyes bore the smoky Nordic inscrutability that has baffled the world's simple-minded males for centuries.

She was my skiing guide for the weekend at a resort in the central Norwegian mountains, a 35-year-old woman named Ann-Therese Barreth. To brief me on the exertions ahead, she drove down from her place in Geilo to join me at dinner in the hotel. She gave the table utter femininity, of course, one which was not especially compromised when she ordered raw beef and rolled her own cigarette.

The November snows had arrived in Geilo a few days before, flocking the birches and pines and presumably shaking the grumpiness out of the trolls, who are supposed to have been the first settlers. A few weeks from now, the skiing regiments would come surging in by the thousands from the offices and kitchens of Oslo and Bergen. But on this day the lifts were dormant and the snow cover was only a half foot deep for cross-country skiing. Yet for a visitor extricating himself from a business trip to Oslo for the weekend, skiing in the highlands of Geilo seemed a reasonable excuse.

Ann-Therese Barreth might have been called a phenomenon back in the middle of the century, a woman horning in on the male dominion of ski guiding. The natives wouldn't classify her that way today. Self-sufficient women are no special oddities anymore among the nomadic ski clans of the world. But when I asked for a local guide, I was expecting the conventional Nordic giant with a blond mustache, red suspenders and a 12-foot stride.

Ann-Therese Barreth displayed no need or ardor for any of these. She closed her schoolroom for the weekend a few hours before, did some interior decorating in the new chalet she owns and built, and drove down the ice chute of a local street to the Bardola Hotel, which is one of the stars of the Geilo mountain resort country.

"Can I introduce an American adventurer to beef tartar?" she asked, ignoring the menu.

The American felt distinctly less venturesome than he did before she ordered. He asked if raw beef gave her verve and iron."

"It gives me relief from cabbage," she said. "Uncooked beef is the only meat I eat. I think it's better for the system, don't you?"

I regarded this woman's slender contours and a face that glistened with vitality. Was I supposed to argue? To spare the chef's feelings, though, I ordered my veal cooked.

She returned an hour after dawn the next morning with my skis and poles, rented from a local shop. I offered a confession and an apology.

"Most of the time when I ski cross-country in America, I do it bushwhacking with a pack on my back," I said. "I've never had much technique. I feel sheepish coming here to the birthplace of cross-country skiing without being able to do a proper Nordic kick and glide."

She dismissed my embarrassment briskly. "Don't give it a second thought, and don't be bothered by it.

"However, you WILL do a proper Nordic kick and glide."

We drove up to the Halstendalen ski area above Geilo, where

the pine groves and clumps of weekend cottages and the cow-sheds yield quickly to a massive, windslapped tundra. Alongside our ski track for nearly a mile, a tumbling brook waged its losing struggle with the encroaching ice. The valley below us seemed lifted from the coffee table photo anthologies, but the plateau was full of wind, cloud and unease. We passed a green-jacketed skiing group working on technique. One of the skiers greeted Ann-Therese and scanned my movements politely.

"They're members of the Norwegian national cross-country ski team," she said, "some of the best skiers in the world.

"Now, if you please, kick and glide."

I kicked and glided. I did it now.

The wind stiffened, tearing the cloud into snags. We skied past a heavy iron railing that guarded the ski track from traffic and moved upward another 45 minutes in the shifting soup. Norway in November. It isn't exactly Spain, but it *is* gripping. She didn't ask if I wanted a breather, and I got the idea I might risk the fury of Thor if I brought it up. Thinking about it, I didn't really need rest. Maybe it was the geography or the reunion with thinner air. Or maybe it was just the suspended judgment of that Norwegian Olympian back down the trail. But I was moving well and under control.

"Good," she said. "I hope you can go downhill, because we take the same track down, and it's fast."

Why die of tedium or suspense? We turned immediately and started down. The wind whistled in my ski cap and the track was slick. From the distant ravines the houses and shops began to enlarge with amazing suddenness. Here and there I even tucked my poles into that underarm waggle you see in the Olympics on TV. Back home I would have snowplowed to save my neck. Here I kept the throttle down, not because I'm brave but because I wanted to stay in sight of the flying lady.

Rounding a turn, I saw a flash of metal ahead.

Oof da, baby. It was the steel guard rail, and it was coming at me like a shot. My options were meager. I could swerve right into a gully, swerve left on a thin ridge of a deep ditch or try to duck under the rail with a Nordic version of the limbo.

I hit for the gully on the right. Unluckily, the points of my skis meshed and flung me to the left. Ann-Therese Barreth looked back in time to see me skimming the knife ridge on one ski, holding the other frantically aloft for balance before the angle of the snow eased enough to slow me down.

"Jeem," she said, "that was good technique. Congratulations."

If she knew the truth, she could have had me deported.

A MOONLIT CRUISE THROUGH THE FJORDS

A woman cocooned in a white ship's comforter sat on the afterdeck of a steamer threading between the 3,000-foot cliffs of Norway's Sogne Fjord.

Except for her visitor emerging from the ship's darkened dining room, she was the only passenger stirring at 2:30 A.M.

"Couldn't you sleep?" I, the visitor, asked.

"I can't imagine who would want to," a voice responded from someplace between the curled comforter and a maroon and gold Minnesota Gophers cap. "It's too incredible to miss."

The hulk of the forested walls on either side of us seemed other-worldly under the violet sky and streaks of metallic cloud. Half a mile away the beacon of a lighthouse slowly rotated on shore. The engines rumbled their pulsing rhythms under us, producing a wake that crashed onto the rocks of the fjord's coastline 50 yards from the ship.

If you want to see Norway you can prowl Oslo and shop for its linens and carvings, or you can walk in the mountain woods. All of which we did. But if you want to feel and understand this place, you must be on the sea.

The sea is Norway's soul and its blood. It has nourished her and engraved its mark on her character, made her both venturesome and vulnerable. It has given the boldest of its people a sense of the beyond, beginning with the time of the longships. To the more stolid ones, it has given a security in the unchanging tide and surf, and what it means to their lives.

The longships are consigned to museums, and the Norwegian migrations of the past hundred years have filled the farms and cities of places like Minnesota. But what Norway can offer best to the world today may be the kind of 48 hours my small troupe spent on its last weekend before home.

At the inland end of the great Sogne Fjord is a hamlet called Fjaerland, the ancestral home of the Fritz Mondale family of Minnesota. Mondale's people called themselves Mundal in Norway. They farmed for generations on the miniature acreage they pried from those two feudal lords of nature in the fjord country, the mountain ice fields and the fjord's salt water. The Mundals ultimately sold their property to the Orheim family, which today operates the 95-year-old Hotel Mundal on a meadowed slope overlooking the Sogne Fjord, Norway's longest and deepest. The hotel is a place of vintage drawing rooms and gourmet cuisine, guest rooms of turn of the century furnishings and marvelous overlooks on the fjord. We had fresh fjord salmon and took our coffee around the piano in the sitting room, watching a slide show lovingly and interminably presented by the proprietor, Alf Orheim.

Listen. Sometimes it's not only okay but absolutely transfixing to travel 6,000 miles to watch a slide show and sip coffee. I admit we had no idea where Orheim's trolls had hidden our boots. He said they were drying them someplace. Early in the day we slogged five hours in the rain to the edge of the 70-mile Jostedal ice field 3,000 feet above the hotel, and came back shipping water to the ankles. But a couple of hours later the men in our clan were wearing jackets and ties, and the women came in gowns brought specially across the Atlantic for this night. You don't have to dress that way in an elderly hotel on a fjord, but why not? Orheim produced our boots in time and we boarded the steamer Firda from the Viking burial mounds at Balestrand a few hours later. For 12 hours we cruised the Sogne Fjord overnight. It was a ride through tunnels of time, following the route of the Norsemen past the villages of Hoyanger, Vadheim and Lavik and into the seaport of Bergen and its tiered row houses from the Hanseatic era above the harbor. They had assigned us sleeping cabins, but how much is sleep worth when you're sailing a fjord under the streamers of the midnight sun?

The reversion of time doesn't mean you are cut off from the here and now. Consumption of grog is not entirely unknown in Norwegian taverns on Saturday nights. We were serenaded by a noisy chorale of local swells at dockside in Vadheim and later by a merciless yodeler. We ate from an endless buffet in the ship's dining room and then watched for hours as the daylight waned but never quite died. At 6:15 A.M. we docked in Bergen and before breakfast walked past the medieval gingerbread of the old town above the waterfront. Vivid colors are big in Scandinavian fashion. The women wore oranges and royal blues and purples, but you didn't see them wearing much of anything on the sun beaches. And that prodded the memory of my one encounter with the Scandinavian mystique. I met her in the laundry room of the mountain hut at Skogasdalboen, where we hiked in the Jotenheimen Mountains. The showers in the next building were cold, so she opted for the cleaning room down the hall.

It was the room where I stopped to fill my water bottle for the next day. She was blond and slender and wearing jeans. That is the beginning and end of the fashion report. She wore nothing above the waist. I do remember gulping obviously and noticing her brilliant tangerine wash cloth. The situation demanded some attempt at urbane conversation. I made a stab at it by saying "hello."

She did the same and went about her business as I filled my water bottle. I had eyes strictly for the faucet. But it still took me three turns of the handle to hit the bottle.

IV.
Going for the Top

Men and women climb mountains for a dozen reasons, some of which they can't fully explain. They don't climb to be miserable, scared or to get hurt. But that happens. They do climb for excitement and replenishment and that, too, comes—weather allowing.

The Matterhorn 30 years apart

Swiss mountain folk are fascinated by the morbidity of climbing. As a fuel for casual gossip, it's fresher than the weather and more variable than the price of cheese.

A few minutes after I stepped off the elfin-red cogwheel railroad train that creaks through a rising valley of waterfalls from the Rhone River to Zermatt, I asked a hotel porter about the summer climbing season.

The porter frowned. "We have four person killed the other day on the Matterhorn. Somebody slip on the ice. Whoosh. It's over."

Swell. Why don't we try the weather?

"Where are you going climbing?" the porter asked with a genuine show of condolence.

"The Matterhorn," I said.

The porter turned out to be a politician. He switched to the psychology of hope and reinforcement. "It's all right," he said. "It should be good. Only fools get killed on the Matterhorn."

I examined that axiom silently. The porter deserved credit for good intentions although probably not for accuracy. I came to terms years ago with the patina of death the historians and village troubadours have laid on the Matterhorn with so much enthusiasm for more than 100 years. Zermatt is one of the few tourist towns I know where the cemetery is a scenic attraction. The tragedy of the first ascent, where the rope broke and launched four climbers to the glacier 4,000 feet below, has become the metaphor of mountain climbing's dicey obsessions.

I climbed the Matterhorn for the first time 30 years ago. When we reached the summit, the cloud was so dense that the iron cross on the Italian side of the summit ridge was invisible. So was my Swiss guide, Gottlieb Perren, until we coiled the rope and performed the mandatory handshakes and division of salami lunch.

If you know about climbing, you are supposed to downgrade the drama of moments like that. Apart from its history, the Matterhorn on the Swiss or northeast ridge is not a climber's climb. Because of that history and because the mountain's sculpture is unique and stunning, climbing the Matterhorn is now a cliché of mountaineering. It is also sometimes an object of in-house disdain in the climbing cult. The traditional Swiss route is not technically demanding. It can be done by anyone with modest experience and in reasonable condition. This assumes there is no sudden tantrum of weather. It also assumes that the mountain on that day will be benevolent when it dumps its random rockfall. It also assumes that the phantoms of the Matterhorn will stay quiet.

None of those conditions is guaranteed. The Matterhorn's weather and rockfall are unpredictable.

As for the ghosts, the obituaries and legends cling so stubbornly that you actually experience the sensation of entering an atmosphere inhabited by the shades of Edward Wymper, Michel Croz and Jean Carrel. Those and dozens of other historic figures who came to the Matterhorn gave the mountain its mixed symbolism as both grail and mausoleum of the climbing urge.

For me, that has always been good and acceptable fairy tale stuff. Even in later years, when I climbed well enough to find more demanding mountains, the Matterhorn remained my one enduring mountaineering romance. It defined the quality of the other climbs. What the porter told me about the latest calamity was essentially the same kind of story I'd heard before each of my six previous climbs on the Matterhorn. That made it oddly comforting. The goblins were still hanging around the Matterhorn's solemn old cliffs. The world was in order and sync.

I thought 30 years was a nice, symmetrical number to measure my passage on the Matterhorn. Climbing a mountain is not the usual recreation one identifies with the age of 60. But it happens to be my recreation, and that happened to be my age. So the idea seemed sensible.

About the aging process, I don't have any great phobias or illusions. People in the ripe middle years and beyond live differently today than 50 years ago. Diets changed. Attitudes changed. Health awareness soared. Leisure time increased and equipment got better. We're more mobile and more eager for the sensations of physical and psychological freedom. We know that if you don't smoke and if you don't drink too much or consume too many fats and use your seat belt and watch your salt, you can do at 60 and 70 approximately what you did at 20 and 30, with the usual allowances. Lastly, like most people, I don't like to see age in the role of autocrat, controlling my agendas and whims.

All of which put me in the Zermatt guide's office in late July. The craggy old retired guide at a desk said my guide on the Matterhorn would be Kurt Ringhofer.

If you have a climbing friend around, climbing the Matterhorn is practically free. If you have to hire a guide, it is hugely expensive. But it is also safe. Climbing the Matterhorn alone is possible but idiotic.

To reach the mountain you can ride the cable car from Zermatt to the Schwartzee Hotel, which is just a two-hour hike to the overnight chalet where the climb begins. But I like to walk with ghosts. I strolled through a platoon of goats on the edge of Zermatt, past the congested colonies of hotels and onto the trail where the Whympers and Carrels made their pilgrimages to the mountain.

Some of the old cowsheds have been preserved. The Arolla pine groves are the same. The adrenalin is the same. The sleek blue cable cars carrying tourists are new, and Wymper would have blinked at the hydroelectric projects and the ski lifts. Yet that enormous black-and-white pyramid of the Matterhorn still floats aloof and inscrutable in the sky. It is still menacing and alluring, a mountain for the imagination. Before I began the final trudge to the overnight hut, I tried to calculate the small erosions of my body over the 30 years. It took me two hours to walk from Zermatt to the Schwartzee in 1958. This time it took me almost three. But you have to understand that I was, ah, more observant. I took more time to linger over the alpine roses, and also to sit on a random rock.

The overnight hotel was bulging with climbers—Japanese, European, American and Australian. Thirty years ago there were five. In 1958 everybody in the hut assumed silent poses of reverence, staring up at the glowering dark hulk of a Matterhorn so close. Tonight, under a full moon, a young man and woman unbashfully made love on the hotel terrace. They had the prudence to store their ice axes, which could have made the exercise awkward.

We were up a 1:00 A.M., and underway 20 minutes later. The summit of this 14,700-foot mountain was nearly a vertical mile away. The eager ones had started well before, imparting to the lower slopes a light show of flickered amber dots created by the moving headlamps. They shone like the candles of medieval acolytes groping toward their own grail.

Kurt and I roped up. We were the oldest team of the day, he said. I had turned off my headlamp earlier. I knew the route from memory. The question was, did my legs and lungs know it.

Before the rocks fell, we were having a romp.

Ringhofer's most endearing quality was his long view of history. "We go steady, the two of us," he said. "Enjoy the climb. Let the young ones race."

As a philosophy of getting from A to Z in the mountains, from the bottom to the top, I've always found this to meet the minimal standards of sanity and self-preservation. On the Matterhorn, it's especially logical. Despite its photogenic appearance, thrusting into the sky like an obelisk of the ages, the mountain is a vast pile of loose rock. The further you remove yourself from somebody's sloppy footwork above you, the better your chances of avoiding a visitor's plot in Zermatt's scenic graveyard. Falling rock is always a hazard on the Matterhorn. About the weather, we had nothing to worry. The morning the sky was a bonfire of starlight and moonlight, and all of the auguries were good.

Kurt was 49, an Austrian. Austrians are not usually found on the rolls of the Swiss alpine huts, where nationalism and family protectionism run pretty fierce. But he is a popular figure in the Matterhorn's guiding menage, gregarious and relaxed and chivalrous. "When you get tired," he said, "tell me and we stop." I remembered Gottlieb Perren using almost identical language on my first climb of the Matterhorn. Gottlieb was austere and precise, the Teutonic temperament in person and lifted into the crags. We climbed together many times, on the Matterhorn's Hornli and Zmutt ridges, and on other mountains. Laughter was not heavily ingrained in Gottlieb's instincts, which didn't bother me because I have never found all that much amusing in a day on the mountain. Bantering and needling are okay. But with Gottlieb it was usually grimness interspersed long gulps of honeyed tea. For me, it was a thrill if we reached the summit, for Gottlieb a mission done. For me it was depression if we didn't, for Gottlieb a dull day at the office.

I don't know how much room ego has occupied in my climbing episodes. There was some of that. But the aging process pretty much dissolves that. In later years I've found it is a good and mostly joyous renewal. It is an exciting hour and a kinship revisited, a freedom rediscovered. I find that climbing in later years still appeases a curiosity, about one's self and the sensation

95

of lifting one's self into the sky. And it never loses one of its first exhilarations—the feeling that you are facing the forbidden because it is a challenge to gravity. The mountain is the old oak tree of our childhood. The wish to climb it is just as primitive. But if you can keep vanity out of it and accept a minimal risk as part of achieving, then climbing can truly make you free, for an hour or for a lifetime.

I felt that less exuberantly but more intimately at 60 than I did at 30 on the Matterhorn. Gottlieb should have been with me, because he's a little looser himself today than he was in 1958. But Gottlieb is making lots of money as a merchant in the valley, and today it was Kurt Ringhofer threading through the sober old chimneys and slag heaps of the Matterhorn's Hornli Ridge. Rod Wilson and I alternated leading the route a few years before, the only time I had done it unaided by a professional guide. Kurt on the rope meant the inevitable travelogue narration, which is part of the guide's craft. He identified the towers and column and glaciers and I kept doing the profuse "yahs" and nods. We went an hour without resting. I was breathing hard but felt no special stress. Most of the rock climb on the Matterhorn is uncomplicated. Once in a while it produces some real exaltation. But the rewards on the Matterhorn have to do not with overcoming some godawful pitch but with feeling the rock and mood of climbing history and mixing your sweat with the memory of climbing's old saints and martyrs.

The young racers were hundreds of yards ahead of us by now, and their guides celebrated the arrival of dawn with a rhapsody of yodels, some of them salty. The yodels drifted down to us from the mountain's buttresses, but more came down than yodels.

"Achtung," a voice bellowed.

It didn't belong to Kurt. He did exactly what I did. We leaned into the wall and got out of the line of the cannonade. Sometimes rock on the Matterhorn falls as splinters and pebbles. Sometimes it is boulders and slabs. From the sound, this one was somewhere in between. Kurt found a deeper crease in the rock than I did. Overhead, the rocks went crump and ping, and a few of them simply exploded as they caromed off the cliffs and disappeared down the east face of the mountain.

Kurt emerged. He was healthy, grinning and helmetless. For a moment I thought a rock might have ripped off his helmet, but then I remembered he was climbing bareheaded. I did have a helmet. I thwacked it vigorously with my right hand when Ringhofer asked if I was all right. I didn't tell him about taking one of the pings above the right ear. As a guide, he would have felt terribly chagrinned if I did. We slipped past the high-angled Mosely slabs beneath the emergency Solvay Hut at 13,500 feet and strapped on our crampons for the snowfields above. We had come nearly 3,000 feet in a little less than three hours. Our progress 30 years before, for whatever significance it had, had been about the same. We sipped tea and started up the snow. There was a momentary traffic jam below the fixed cables that protect the climber on the exposed North Face. It gave me a chance to do some decent reminiscence. What had happened in 30 years? Trying to be both charitable and honest, I found myself mulling a proverb about an old hunting shack in the mountains not far from here. I didn't translate the German perfectly, but it said something close to this: "Good luck and bad luck, carry them both with peace. All of it will pass, and so it will be with you."

Well, that may not have sent my heart soaring. The Matterhorn's summit, cold and radiant like a huge gemstone, came closer to doing that. In a few minutes we were on top. The mountain's summit ridge is a long frozen wave of white, broken by cracks in the cornices. The iron cross on the Italian side was being pelted by a small whirlwind of spindrift. The wind on the Swiss side cut into the nose and cheeks, and I made the usual mental genuflections on the Matterhorn summit hurried and brief. But they were earnest.

People argue about what are the realities of life. I don't know if making money, watching ball games, paying bills and dealing with relatives is any more real than walking the summit ridge of the Matterhorn with the west wind in your face and the sun on your skin and Kurt Ringhofer stretching out his hand.

"Was good, my friend," he said. It was. And when I got back to the Hornli Hut, my wife waved a salute. And the day and the years seemed to join.

"Jimmy," the guide said in the hut over his beer, "is a good reason to wear the helmet."

They could make a song out of that and outsell the yodels.

Grappling with the Devil

John Peterson's helmet crumpled into a vertical slab high on the Devil's Tower. It sounded like a small bomb.

He was stunned and motionless, held upright by the tension of the protective climbing rope, a 66-year-old man with knickers and a highly developed gift for finding improbable predicaments for a Golden Ager. His arms were wrapped around a flake of rock jutting above the vertical slab where he lost his footing.

Doug Kelley and I called down to him for the casualty report. There was no answer.

"John," I said, "if you can help yourself, there's a place to sit a few feet above you."

The white helmet began to stir, casting reflected spears of sunlight that seemed to communicate a restored energy. John's leggy frame slowly shifted position in the rope harness. He brought one hand around the back of the helmet, evidently to discover the source of the horde of bumblebees zinging in his ears. His fingers tried without much conviction to signal an all's-well greeting.

Kelley cheered. "Come on up when you're ready," he said. "We have food and friendship."

Neither seemed especially persuasive to John Peterson. It was not a matter of ingratitude. The problem was the bumblebees. John had no idea of where he was sitting, what century he was occupying or the identity of those odd people calling down at him. But eventually he made his way to a rock platform, from which we belayed him up to us, and he sat to reorganize himself. His eyes were clear but his memory was a bog of black tunnels and dead ends.

"Do you know what mountain we're on," one of us asked.

John marshalled a kinky smile. "Make it multiple choice," he said.

He speculated that 15 minutes would be enough for him to unscramble the mystery. He appeared to be in no pain, but he understood the implications of the accident without illusions. If he hadn't been wearing the helmet, he might still be plastered on the flake and he would be solving no riddles today.

We offered him some Gatorade to relieve his sandpaper tongue.

His eyes explored the 1,000-foot fluted wall of the rock chimney that shoots so grotesquely out of the otherwise sensible prairie and pine forests of eastern Wyoming.

The Devil's Tower is not a true mountain. It is nature's revenge against the unending prairie. It is a stone gray mutant on the green and buff landscape, a geological renegade thrusting mute and preposterous above the grazing carpets of the Belle Fourche River Valley. There is nothing in any direction to prepare the traveler for it. It is baffling and hypnotic. What was nature up to here? What forces did it conjure to create this obelisk hulk, grooved so precisely from top to bottom for its entire girth that it seems almost machined.

At the moment, Peterson was not much absorbed by these curiosities. But the bogs in his mind started to thin. He remembered eating a steak the night before at the Aro Cafe in Sundance and mediating a 100-mile argument across the South Dakota plain in which the lawyer (Kelley) and the journalist (me) exchanged thunderbolts over a recent Supreme Court decision allowing police to rummage in newsrooms. In it, John intruded now and then. Characteristically, he argued both sides with great passion and precision before his Republican ancestry exposed his true bias. The fourth member, Rod Wilson, also a lawyer, nodded sagely at the right times and was generally accorded the role of judge. After a hundred miles he gave a verdict. "If you're finished, let's eat."

John remembered that. And he ultimately remembered trying a route not in the guide book, coming off the rock and bouncing into the slab.

But he was clearheaded again in a few minutes, and we resumed. The custodians of Devil's Tower keep no longevity records, yet it's not easy to imagine many other 66-year-olds having come this far on a climb so arduous. We liked him for it, not so much for his zest in trying or even for his indomitability. What we like most was John's balanced view of age, mortality and joy. Age doesn't mean you have to close the door to excitement and discovery, or even to a manageable risk. But age also brings you closer to the beyond, and John remembered all of that. It didn't prevent him from trying a new route. But it reminded him to wear the helmet and to climb with mountaineers, Kelley and Wilson, who were half his age and strong but prudent. I was somewhere between them, which probably made us one of the oldest parties at the time ever to venture onto the Tower. It was the reason, in fact—spawning an impulse which John and I shared—that put us on the mountain.

So, it seems, there is nothing wrong with asking yourself at 66, or 50, if you have the command of your body to achieve a Devil's Tower, an undertaking that creates symbols both physical and psychological. It would be wrong only if, in trying to get there, you were goaded by some idea of a chest-pounding elite. A rock climb with that in mind is a stunt. A day on the hard rock in the sun ought to be a day to remember, and it doesn't have to be much more. Add to that a celebration of age in a pretty bizarre setting, and you ought to be ready to trade off some discomfort and a little pain for the sensation of movement and shared excitement. How about inviting risk? It's one of those shadowy parts of the equation that belongs in there somewhere. But it's a minor part for the recreational climber who knows his or her limits and understands the uncompromising principles of gravity.

Some people ask, "Why do it?" with skepticism, some contemptuously and some with actual curiosity. Climbers usually flounder in answering because the truth sometimes embarrasses them, or because the truth is not the same for everyone, not always easy to find and not easy to synthesize. The satisfaction of climbing a rock route may not be far removed from the satisfaction the successful chess player feels. Begin with a problem. Chart its solution. Visualize yourself two or three moves ahead. Stay in control. Understand what you are capable of doing, and what you are not.

But that is the mathematics of it. The inner jubilance comes on places like the Durrance Crack of the Devil's Tower, when the climber discovers he has the strength and rhythm in his body, whatever his age, and something inexplicable in his glands to blend with the elements. When he learns that he can work his way through the chimney and surmount the hardest parts technically, then the stresses dissolve, and it really becomes a carol.

The student pianist may recognize the feeling. She prepares for weeks for her recital. While giving it, she plays with tension and not much joy. Tomorrow morning the tension is gone but the technique is still fresh, and she can play and play, freely and at the limit of her abilities.

Moments like that may not occur often, but they're worth the sweat and the hairiness. They produce a purification.

But before they did, we had to get past the Durrance Crack, a 72-foot column and vertical crevice above a broken tower, running straight up and down. It is the crux of the climb. Kelley,

102

leading, was wrestling with it above us, forcing his right foot into a three-inch-wide seam, gripping a vertical slab with his outstretched arms as he inched upward, his left foot barely making contact with a second crack on the left. He jammed his fist into that seam, using it for leverage as he gained altitude. He did it efficiently and flawlessly. John followed. He was breathing heavily a third of the way up, and slipping occasionally. Three times he had to lower himself to a point 30 feet above the start of the crack. Once he stopped for five minutes to breathe and to quiet the trembling in his muscles. Years before he had climbed this route almost without effort. John was one of those effervescent, willful, goal-setters, a salesman and an honest-to-God Dale Carnegie instructor in his volunteer hours. He was also a remarkable powerful man of six-foot-four, bony and bald. He had climbed this route a half dozen times, on the first attempt each time, and now he found himself stymied. His long fingers searched the smooth rock above him for tiny ledges and nubs. But he knew they weren't there, and sooner or later he had to go back into the cracks with his fingers and use his toes for friction.

It probably did not occur to John D. Peterson that he might be too old to be climbing the Devil's Tower.

Which did not necessarily mean that he *wasn't* going to climb the Devil's Tower.

From below I tried to do some spying for him, picking out a route he might not be able to see. Rod joined, and in a few moments we were a noisy claque, telling John what a marvelous job he was doing in the Durrance Crack.

The old Carnegie man looked down and laughed archly. But he went back to the rock and in ten minutes he was standing with Doug. An hour later he was grappling with bumblebees, but the last 400 feet were a frolic.

We scrambled to the top quickly, because the afternoon was wearing on and rain clouds were building up in the west. We strolled a grassy ledge called The Meadows and then scooted the easy final pitches to the broader meadow on top.

We did the usual candy bars and pictures there and then roped down, arriving just as the rain struck at sunset. When we untied on the bottom, John Peterson supervised the housekeeping, distributing ropes and hardware and separating packs.

"John," I said, "congratulations. It was a pleasure again. If you had it to do over, would you change anything?"

John's bald old head emerged from his ropes. He was mugging, and he looked like a mischievous bald eagle, which isn't easy. "Yeah," he said. "I'd change my helmet. This one picked up a helluva crack somewhere."

A gale and hallucination in the Andes

His eyes declared all the symptoms of acute high-altitude sickness. They were glazed and lethargic, barely reactive to work and movement.

He tried to sit up in his sleeping bag but sank back onto the tent floor, defeated by exhaustion and by the Andean night wind that contorted the tent's fiberglass poles and deflated its walls.

The wind needed no resort to the sound effects of terror, no shrieking or orchestral tantrums. It was constant and inescapable. This was its dominion, at 19,000 feet in the frozen cascades and glacier fields of the Cordillera Blanca in the Peruvian Andes. Those who intruded accepted that as a condition of their brief and tenuous habitation. It was nonnegotiable.

In spite of the wind, you could hear Rod Wilson gagging and snuffling.

A few minutes before, he awoke the native porter, Fausto, and me. He did it by sitting up and nudging me with his foot, and by speaking in a voice that seemed drained of all animation and yet possessing a toneless, bizarre dignity and a thread of apology.

Rod Wilson said he was dying.

He said there was water in his lungs; he could hear himself gurgling when he tried to breathe. He didn't know where he was and he felt himself drifting. He said he had to tell us.

I put a flashlight on Rod's face and pulled the stethoscope out of our first aid pouch. To get acquainted with our bodies' norms, we had listened to each other's heartbeats and breathing rhythms a half dozen times—Rod, Doug Kelley, and I. The first time was in the Monterrey Hotel room in Huaraz at 9,500 feet and at the overnight camps thereafter on the route to Nevado Huascaran, a mountain whose summit rises 22,200 feet above the sea.

A critical hazard on a mountain so high is pulmonary edema, a condition brought on by inadequate acclimatization to thin atmosphere, and characterized in part by gurgling in the lungs when the victim breathes.

Rod's face was gray, puffed, and expressionless. It revealed neither fright nor pain. I put the stethoscope under his lungs and on his back. I don't know how the medical people define gurgling in the lungs. I heard a crackling when Rod breathed. I had no training to judge its severity. I did know he was disoriented and, from the events of the day, dehydrated and ground out. Rod's own frail diagnosis of his condition seemed accurate. Listless and hallucinatory, he looked like a man about to die. There was a medicine capsule in my hand, and a hypodermic needle. I broke off the top of the capsule with a pair of pliers and extracted the medicine with the syringe.

Rod rolled over face down, and I emptied the needle in his bottom. He didn't cringe, flinch, or groan. he said, "Thanks, doc," and lost consciousness.

And then Fausto Milla strapped on his crampons and crawled out of the tent to begin a 5,000-foot descent through the night wind and glacial crevasses for an oxygen bottle at the base camp a millennium away.

Have you seen the Andes?

Where the Rockies peak out, the Andes's everlasting snow and ice are just beginning. They ride in the sky above the jungle and above the sea in their startling architecture, an Alpamayo that flings its summit to the sun like a white diamond, a Copa with its symmetry of connected peaks laced together with ice ridges that give it the look of some celestial suspension bridge.

And Huascaran. The highest in Peru, although hardly the prettiest. Actually a double mountain separated by a high saddle at 19,000 feet called La Garganta, the gate to its ascent either on the north side or the true summit to the south, Huascaran Sur. It has the classic contours of the conical mountain, but it is too immense to be loved. Climbing Huascaran, unless one encounters a storm or loses the route, does not demand gymnastic technique. In some places it is a slog and a grunt, although in others it offers the airiest kind of pleasure to the mountaineer under control. And yet it is not especially forgiving.

Doug, Rod, Fausto, a young porter named Jacinto, and I clambered up the glacier's lateral moraine from Camp One, strapped on our crampons, and walked onto the ice, carrying packs.

It was a supernatural place.

We walked among great blue grottos and amphitheaters, icicles 50 feet long, crevasses 300 feet deep. The Andean sun blazed them into a concerto of turquoise, amethyst, and cobalt. The Patagonia pile we wore already was steaming, so we removed that and scaled down to two sets of underwear and moisture-resistant Gore-Tex pants and jackets.

The sun burned through the glacial cream but we were moving higher and higher, leaping the crevasses and listening to the avalanches rolling down Huascaran North, and I could not help remembering George Patton: "God forgive, I love it so."

And in time we would love Fausto Milla.

He called us amigos.

His scrambled, breakneck Spanish and highland patois could not accommodate the names of Doug, Rod, and Jim, and his English was an outright surrender. His copper face was a recon-

107

ciliation of the races of man, reflecting the broken visions and struggles of the centuries, the elfin innocences and the leathered wariness. Yet for all that he was bouncy and sociable. His ancestries sprang from the islands of the mid-Pacific, the Indian clans that flowed from them, the Spanish gold-diggers who conquered them, and the undefined nations that gave his features a timeless universality.

He was listed in the expedition registries of the Andes as a guide-porter, but this was shamelessly inadequate. He was also part burro and part roadrunner. He had the undefeatable tinkerer's soul of a garage mechanic down to his last cotter pin in the house. He smiled with the simple radiance of the rising sun and he was the lodge morale man in the tent, quizzing his clients about their love lives and their gastronomic prejudices. But on his home terrain, the glaciers of the Cordillera Blanca, he was despotic and rude. If you hired Fausto Milla to escort you through the crevasses, perish something as offensive as an original thought.

Moreover, he carried a ton.

There was practically nothing in the smorgasbord of camping and mountaineering gear that could not be borne, voluntarily and eagerly, on Fausto Milla's back. He was 32 and could not have weighed more than 135 pounds, but there were days when he carried close to a hundred. If you proposed to relieve him of a few of those, Fausto Milla scowled and dismissed the suggestion as the addled notion of a tenderfoot. As a climber he was sure and brave, but dangerously primitive in his rope management techniques and his conceptions of ax work.

Beyond all, he was an amigo, a friend, almost always optimistic but, at the critical times, direct. He wanted to reach the summit, but it was still a day's work if he didn't. It all depended, he said, on tiempo, the weather.

Tiempo mal mañana," he would say each evening, "aqui."

If the weather is bad tomorrow, if it is too cloudy in the La Garganta high saddle or an Andean hurricane is blowing on the route to Nevado Huascaran, we stay in the tent.

"Tiempo bueno mañana, arriba."

If it's good, we climb.

"Tiempo mal dos, tres dias, abajo." A virtuoso performance with the fingers accompanied this announcement.

If it's bad for two or three days, we go down.

The equation was compact and impossible to misunderstand.

But there was one other part in it that had nothing to do with the tiempo.

Doug Kelley was mal, which is to say he was queasy and inert.

In his natural ambience, Kelley is a sportive, chattering man-about-the-world, filled with the confident lawyer's wit and irreverence and the ex-Green Beret's pride in his musculature and stamina. He is also one of the best climbers in the northern United States, a sophisticate in the use of all the Yosemite rock-climber's jangling hardware.

None of that opens doors in the Andean stratosphere. The reaction of the body to its thin air, especially with limited acclimatization, is unpredictable.

An Adirondack backpacker might go as high as the jets.

A muscle beacher might fall into a stupor 7,000 feet below him.

Doug was laboring at 16,000 feet, grabbing for air, his insides already knotted from an unsuccessful bout with breakfast at Camp One's 14,600 feet.

He upbraided himself and searched for explanations.

By the time we reached Camp Two high on the glacier at 17,000 feet— exactly a mile beneath Huascaran's south summit— he was dragging.

He struggled against the nausea and torpor sucking him down, tried first to overpower it and then outtalk it.

For the three days we were weathered in at Camp Two, Kelley scarcely took solid nourishment. He pretended. He was sly. He would grab a couple of spoonfuls and then walk around the tent unsteadily, dumping the rest of the contents of his canteen when

109

he thought nobody was observing.

His compadres observed.

He would wake up in the morning announcing he had experienced a miraculous rehabilitation. But he almost never left the tent, and his face began swelling under the eyes. His lips were thick and crusted and he looked consummately miserable and sick.

Doug struggled into his climbing clothes on Saturday, made an obligatory but futile try at breakfast, and then sat on his pack, distant from the others.

"Take what you need from my gear," he said finally. "I'm going down. I'm too weak to climb, and there's no use holding you up."

He did not sound or look very heroic, but a climber will understand the fundamental sacrifice. He might have invoked, indirectly or silently, some musketeer's code requiring all of us to go down and await his recovery. Big expeditions would never entertain that indulgence, but there were only three of us on Huascaran, and we had nurtured the climb for months.

We thanked him with respect and concern, and he wobbled off down the glacier with Jacinto, much of his equilibrium gone.

Above Camp Two vaulted the technical crux of the climb, a 450-foot icefall where the glacier broke over a series of rock cliffs. Wilson and I roped with Fausto and began chopping a route up the wall with our axes and crampons. Halfway up it occurred to me that Wilson's bad leg must make this exercise painfully awkward. He had wrenched his knee six weeks before, jumping out of a canoe, and it was still stiff.

I asked him about it on the icefall, and got the same tape-recorded answer he had been giving us for weeks.

"Good," he said.

"That's some summation for a lawyer," I said.

"It was the best I could do on short notice," he said.

We cleared the icefall, waded hip-deep in soft, ascending

snow for an hour, and then encountered the Garganta's predictable gales a half hour before reaching Camp Three.

The winds had accelerated to something close to 60 miles an hour by the time we reached the campsite at 19,000 feet, still at least one day and 3,200 feet below the summit. Pitching Kelley's dome tent under these conditions compared in raw aggravation with installing an overcoat on a three-armed man. When you got part of the fabric under control, a loose end would billow and flap and threaten to launch all three of us into the stratosphere.

By 6:00 P.M. we had eaten the chef's specialty (mine), freeze-dried beef Stroganoff from the shelves of Midwest Mountaineering, and were snugly fortified against the wind.

While the nylon crashed and the fiberglass poles twisted and doubled, I lay in my bag, taking an inventory.

The night before a high climb is a time for that. It should avoid melodrama but still acknowledge that this is an alien place for man, of the unknown and of hazard that could never be completely controlled. So that there was some remote chance of this being a last night on Earth, and therefore a time for summing up. I gave thanks for the good that had come to me, and hoped that whatever good I had done overscaled the injuries I had inflicted, and the neglect. I thought of those close to me, summoned their faces and the best of our times, and I experienced both love and regret, but when I finished I was content.

The wind subsided by morning. It was going to be a gaudy winter's day in the Andes and it was going to be hot despite the four-mile altitude.

Wilson said he was eager and ready, and established this beyond all dispute by throwing up his breakfast.

We were going for the summit, lofting above us, silver and metallic, in arpeggios of ice cliffs. But we weren't going very fast. After one hour we were heaving for air with almost every stride, Wilson and I, fighting the 20,000-foot altitude. In two hours we had to resort to grubby goals: Twenty-five strides, and then breathe for a minute. Maybe two, or three. Wilson, trudging behind me, was tiring. His leg, partly. His malaise from early morning, partly. But Fausto Milla, in his Cordillera wisdom, had decided on the additives needed to get us to the top: a heavy supper the night before. Eat everything in sight. We tried. What about water? The gringos weren't raised in the Cordillera or the Incans' adobe. They needed at least four quarts of liquid a day to keep going.

And Fausto Milla had packed a one-quart plastic canteen of water, for three people, for a 3,200-foot ascent, and descent, on a hot winter's day four miles above the sea in the Andes Mountains.

Some climbers get sustenance out of snow. Wilson does not. At 21,000 feet he asked for lip balm. I pulled a tube of Lip Ivo out of my pocket and, absently studying it, discovered for the first time that the raspberry-flavored ointment we had been smearing on our lips was manufactured in Minneapolis. Alms from Hiawatha. This high sun ignited the snowfields and flung the glare and thermal power into our goggled faces. Fausto and I swabbed another layer of zinc oxide, and Wilson drenched himself in some high-powered sun screen. The track was firm, but endless. How high is the sky?

We resumed.

Now we were down to 20 strides and recuperation. When Wilson sucked in all the air he could, he called "yo," and we moved again. Fausto Milla seemed annoyed and impatient, as though we might be needlessly goldbricking, and he tugged at the rope. I yanked it the other way and cursed. I walked up to him and jabbed a finger into his chest. "We're gringos," I said, "going as fast as we can. If we can't breathe, we can't walk." Fausto grinned sympathetically. I apologized. The little man was still an amigo.

At 4:05 P.M. we mounted the little snow dais decorated with orange flags left by an Austrian team and stood on the summit of Nevado Huascaran, 22,200 feet above the sea. We hugged Fausto Milla and said, "Gracias."

112

Some gringos were crazy and some were obsessed, Fausto said in Spanish, and he wasn't sure where we belonged.

"These," I said, "are not obsessed. They are just tired."

Summit attitudes on a big mountain usually do not make good theater. No one I know falls to his knees to worship the view, although the view may be extraordinary, as it was here at the zenith of the Cordillera Blanca on a day when the sun bejeweled a whole congregation of gigantic peaks. The architecture was numbing. It assembled white pyramids, obelisks, massive domes, and elegant massifs spun together by ridges of glistening blue ice.

Mostly you feel relief and gratitude.

I told Rod Wilson he deserved the summit more than anyone I knew. He nodded in appreciation but seemed momentarily to disagree. Dehydrated and ailing, he decided not to risk the exertion of a reply. What he was doing with his remaining mental acuities was figuring out ways he could prolong the delays downward. It is a wily art founded on sheer survival instinct. It might or might not matter that the others on the rope are aware of the techniques. Let them breathe on their own time.

Fausto was preceding us on the rope at the most dangerous time of any strenuous climb, the downward drag when the elations and anticipations have receded and the drudgery and fatigue-fed complacencies take over. He was showing the way, but he should have been doing it from the last position on the rope, not the first, the better to belay or secure in case of a slip.

We reached a high-angled ice sheet that required front-pointing with the teeth of the crampons and simultaneous leverage with the ice ax. Fausto was 25 feet below me and well to the left. The rope was looped tight around his imbedded ax, but he was in no position to exert immediate tension on the rope in the event of a fall.

The front points of my crampons gave way and I started to slide.

I dug the pick of the ax into the slope, but kept sliding, 25 feet, until the ax stopped the unwilling glissade.

Fausto and I glared at each other.

"Christos," I said.

Fausto grinned. "I had it," he was saying, "all the way."

All the way to where?

So now Rod, limping and fatigued, began his descent, his rope looped around my ax. Five feet down the slope, he lost control, and then his ax.

There could be no tension on the rope to arrest his skid for at least 35 or 40 feet. He streaked down the ice, struck an overhang and shot onto a lower slope with an 800-foot runout.

As he did I drove my shoulders into the ax and buried it to the pick.

The rope came taut, and held.

And his ax came down in Rod's lap.

We called once, and got no response. Again.

Rod lifted an arm. I cramponed down to check him out. To reach him I had to make a long step over a snowbridge.

A snowbridge over what, it occurred to me?

Over a crevasse. It was four feet wide and it was walled in incredible blue and it must have reached halfway to Peking.

In tumbling down the overhang, Rod has missed falling into one of the deepest crevasses on the mountain.

He dusted off and kept plodding downward. A hundred strides, then gulp air. Swab on some lotion, anywhere. The face, the wrists, only do it very fastidiously to buy more time.

He never complained. But it was taking forever. By nightfall we were still nearly an hour above the Garganta's plateau and Camp Three just below it. Fausto had lost all of his impatience and was generous and thoughtful at the sound of Rod's wheezes. We got off the slope and were now walking the plateau toward camp, toward a conflagration of stars, toward the Southern Cross.

There wasn't a whisper of wind, almost uncanny for this hour and this geography, where the usual powerful wind might have finished Rod.

We had neighbors. A low-slung little tent and two larger ones. We got Rod into the tent and removed his crampons and boots. Fausto started the Optimus inside the tent, which is not enthusiastically recommended by tent makers or tent dwellers, but the conditions were not normal.

Rod took two sips of soup and turned down everything else. He was asleep in two minutes. At 11:00, with the wind rising, he awoke us, ashen and gagging, and said he thought he was dying from pulmonary edema.

Fausto got ready to descend 5,000 feet to Camp One for the oxygen tank we stored there, at Doug Kelley's suggestion. In the adjacent tent was another native porter and his client, a television photographer from Cincinnati. Fausto persuaded the porter to descend with him. While he did, I rummaged around the rest of the tiny village, looking for help. In the low-lying tent were an experienced Swiss climber and his girlfriend, equipped with more pertinent medical stores than we had. The Swiss volunteered medicine he said was useful for malaria victims and might do something for Rod's blood and circulation.

Fausto was just leaving when I made the injection.

"You have to hurry," I said. "I know it is not easy going down from the Garganta at night, but he may die unless the oxygen is here by afternoon."

Fausto and the other porter began their descent shortly after 11:00 P.M., in strong winds and full moon. It was at least three hours to Camp Two at normal pace and another two to Camp One. Allowing 15 minutes to a half hour there, plus seven to eight more hours for the return ascent, I calculated Fausto could not return with the oxygen until at least one or two in the afternoon.

Rod drank some hot chocolate at 7:00 A.M. but in movement and speech he was fogged and disoriented, a zombie who did not want to impose. He spoke tonelessly to people who weren't there and talked about the impending try for the summit, vowing he was strong enough to make it. By now he must have lost at least 20 pounds.

I had scooped out a fresh batch of ice and snow to boil on the Optimus shortly before 10:00 A.M. when somebody twanged, "Hey gringo."

Fausto Milla materialized with the crate of oxygen.

Imagine.

Down perpendicular ice walls in the middle of the night past Camp Two, threading crevasses unroped on the two-mile-wide glacier. More than 5,000 feet vertically to Camp One, and then retrace.

He had done it all in less than half a day, three and four hours ahead of what I thought was a reasonable timetable.

I unhooked the crate and handed Rod the nosepiece.

Pure oxygen flowed into his lungs for 30 minutes.

"Is bueno (good)?" Fausto asked Rod Wilson. He was fraternal, worried, an amigo.

"Bueno," Wilson said.

He took oxygen at intervals for the next two hours, and then we roped up with two relief porters from Camp One for the descent of the icefall.

His pulse was close to normal by the time we reached Camp Two, and at Camp One the next day, he was eating again. We conscripted a horse for Rod on the descent to Musho, and learned there that the proprietor of the little cafe on the dusty main street was Fausto Milla himself.

His cook came with hot soup and rolls, with an entrée of rice and creole sauce and sautéed chicken. There were meats in the soup that were sweet but palatable, and I didn't have the nerve to ask their origin but I know they weren't beef, pork, or veal, or anything close.

"El condor pasá, Fausto," I said with some vague philosophical urge.

"Si," he said gravely.

116

I went outside, extracted my ice ax from the pack, and handed it to Fausto. Rod did the same with his glacier glasses. The Peruvian's brown eyes expanded and shone. Behind him was a little Indian girl with her bright costume and shawl and funny square hat, for whom I had plucked a flower on our way into Musho.

She had a flower for me.

And it occurred to me that one little native girl's smile can melt much snow and ice, and sometimes the best and most enduring discoveries do not require an ascent of 22,000 feet.

V.
The Hidden Doors of Yellowstone's Theater

Millions know the geysers and painted pools. The bears are synonymous with it. In winter, Yellowstone changes faces and colors, and then it is wildlife and steam and a hundred things more. To find its soul in summer as well as in winter, though, you have to go beyond the shows and sounds.

Earthquake in a Frosty Oasis

The earth rattled beneath us a few hours after we entered a phantasmal oasis in the middle of Yellowstone's Hayden Valley in February.

We had emerged through a heavy snowshower into emerald meadows and vapor in the midst of the spreading snowfields. And if that were not eerie enough, here was a dull rumbling and shaking somewhere within the volcanic innards of the place.

We felt it as we lay in our tents. But none of us asked the question that must have raced through the minds of all four: Did it start this way in 1959, when a major quake tore up the Hebgen Dam, killed tourists and altered the chemistry of Yellowstone for centuries to come?

Yellowstone in winter is a geological soap opera in which the scenes and characters move chaotically through an identity crisis. They are scenes that seem to be worked out by a moody choreographer who is moved both by mischief and genius. The traveler can ski on a deep snowpack in below-zero weather and discover a steamy grassland and arboretum nourished by hot springs. Colonies of mites and brine flies whirl in orbit above a thermal vent nearby. The mites' lifestyle has a limited radius. If they deviate three inches from orbit, they are blotto, stiff on the ground.

The oasis was described on the maps as Highland Hot Springs but for hours it was a mirage. We were floundering in snow up to the navel, sweating under the sun's brief midday appearance and groping for the route to Mary Lake somewhere on the fringes of Hayden Valley.

All right, why were we crossing the Hayden Valley of Yellowstone in February, when even grizzlies take the season off and get lost in some handy den?

Lord, why not? If there is something in the wilderness that reaches to the deepest glands of curiosity, it follows that winter itself is the last wilderness left in today's head-for-the-hills propulsions in summer. You can't blame people for wanting the lakes and parks in summer. But if you want to avoid congestion, you have to come to terms with winter. And there is no winter like the one in the roadless heartland of Yellowstone. The geological ages come together, and geyser spray frosts the trees with Christmas flocking. The buffalo evoke the age of dinosaurs, plodding beside streams where trumpeter swans float like snow queens.

Not far away, a petrified forest thrusts its strange statuary above the snowfield. No one who has been to Yellowstone in winter will ask why come there in winter.

Our party was small but experienced and reasonably sound psychologically. Bill Stang was a carpenter and contractor from Minneapolis—shrewd, earthy and weathered—one of those creatures who finds joy prowling in isolation. He was bearable. Doug Kelley was bearable despite being a super-efficient onetime Green Beret and a former government prosecutor. Rod Wilson was bearable despite his practice of snoring in the tent. And I was presumed to be bearable despite a number of social quirks.

"How come you don't talk more on the trail?" Bill Stang asked.

"I try to concentrate on breathing," I said honestly.

En route to Mary Lake we were halfway to Old Faithful on our five-day trek. A herd of buffalo stared dolefully at us from the banks of a steaming creek at the bottom of a slope. They looked prehistoric and dimly menacing. But we were less scared than jealous. The buffalo occupied the opposite side of the river, which was our destination. The problem here was the crossing. There wasn't any. The first salvation for a predicament like that in Yellowstone is a snowbridge, which has to be tested carefully. The next option is a helpful log. No such gifts were in view. After reconnoitering for hundreds of yards, we found enough clumps of hardened lava to hop across in our ski boots. A little green terrace liberated by the stream's gases was an ideal place to picnic. But it played pranks on our ski bottoms, which picked up gobs of snow the next two hours. Wilson lifted his ski once to discover a foot-thick slab of snow glued to the tail. I banged my ski pole against Wilson's ski, repeating a maneuver I performed a hundred times on my own skis. It was a fiberglass pole, plenty durable. But clearly it was not unbreakable. It cracked six inches from the tip.

There are worse calamities than a broken ski pole on a mountain trek, where every stride needs leverage and support. But there aren't many. Stang and I examined the wreckage. Stang is the final refinement of the do-it-yourself society, a man who could have fixed the Titanic with a hot patch and a pair of pliers. He turned my mess kit knife into a splint and strapped it to the pole with duct tape. When the duct tape was gone, we used adhesive tape. When Stang was finished, the pole worked. And when Stang had vanished down the slopes, I examined the other pole.

It was broken six inches from the tip.

By the time I reached the orange blazes denoting the route into the timber and toward Mary Lake, I was the only skier in the Rockies carrying his knife on one pole and his fork on the other.

It was not the most scenic equipment, but it was functional. And the poles were still intact when suddenly the snows parted and through a whorl of mist we entered the pastures and sinter beds of Highland Hot springs.

You have to buck miles of snow and tent in it night after night to appreciate the raw luxury of Highland Hot Springs. The normal procedure in setting up a tent in snow is to pack the tent site for a half hour, hopping around on skis to create a platform. And when you get off your skis to prepare the bedding, you sink to the crotch in soft snow until it hardens from use. But at Highland Hot Springs, we found grass soft and deep enough for a cows' picnic. The night was warm and friendly, and a few hundred feet away a fumarole sputtered and sang.

"All we need is an apple and a serpent," somebody said.

Fifteen minutes later we felt the first rumble. The feet seemed to tingle and the movement rippled through the body. It was a shock, a faint one. The tremor continued. Something deep below us seemed to be surging slowly, and we stared at each other, because once every generation or so a quake will hit Yellowstone with a destructive force.

But in a matter of seconds the vibrations ended.

In the geologist's office at Old Faithful 20 miles away, they were recorded on the seismograph, one of 18 to 20 annually registered on the Richter Scale there. But this was the only Yellowstone tremor reported so far this year, the seismic watchers reported later. They logged it officially at 2.5, but offered wry congratulations: "It happened just a few hundred yards from where a 6.1 earthquake happened in 1975, and shook rocks and dust all over the Grand Canyon of the Yellowstone. You were standing right over the epicenter."

But there was no destruction on this night. Relieved, Doug Kelley strode to a snow-covered log, which he deemed qualified to serve as his forum for the evening meal. Kelley anointed himself the supper chef early in the trip. He is a man of fastidious dining habits for a lawyer, and he did not argue with the group's consensus that he was a helluva cook with Rich-Moor's freeze-dried food.

Kelley looked on his kitchen duties, therefore, with a sense of noblesse oblige. If a man is good, why suppress it? Where most winter cooks will slap a pot on the Optimus stove, boil some water and pour it into the foil bags, Kelley spends time carefully crafting shelves and counters in the snow, reasoning that you wouldn't ask a violinist to give a concert in a junkyard.

For tonight he chose beef Stroganoff, preceded by chicken-flavored noodle soup. It brought the expected sighs of adulation from his guests. But when one leaned against the snow shelf for support, Kelley scowled.

"You're about to sit in the dessert."

"I don't see any dessert."

"It's in that foil bag. It's lemon pie."

Kelley's companion boorishly stared into the aluminum bag.

"I just see yellow glop."

"For God's sake, it's settling. Give it a half hour and it will harden into pie. And don't sit on the rest of the dessert."

The boor peered into another foil bag.

"It's just brown powder."

"It's Graham cracker crumbs," Kelley corrected. "Just let me work, will you?"

The boor retired in proper disgrace. Actually, Kelley's blueberry cobbler the night before was pretty lousy.

I would never have confronted him with that. He might have handed the apron and the spatula to me.

Which is a sure ticket to starvation.

A WALK ON THE FAR SIDE
OF YELLOWSTONE

The most famous fuming sideshows on earth are not easy to resist. But on some days they should be resisted, to allow for a glimpse of the far side of Yellowstone.

Yellowstone invites the tourist armies. It does that without blushing, and why not? It is a sensational place with its thermal carnivals and its profusion of wildlife. Millions mob the geyser basins and pastel pools each year. They come to view the most celebrated of all natural prima donnas, Old Faithful. They come for petrified forests and for bears and moose and for the pure immensity of it. It rarely disappoints them, although the park's custodians had to undertake a major shift in policy two decades ago to rescue Yellowstone from smothering traffic jams and the chaos of an asphalt zoo.

It was then when the government re-located hundreds of mooching bears into the park interior and rebuilt the highways to reduce congestion around the scenic extravaganzas.

With that came the return of comparative peace and order, and a Yellowstone closer to the great wildlife preserve and forest playground that its founders visualized. Yet the interior of Yellowstone remains unknown to most of the invading multitudes who come, ironically, to find some relief from the crunches of modern life.

It shouldn't be that hard to find. The far side of Yellowstone, the infrequently visited interior, stretches for miles in all directions and is eminently reachable by most highways.

There is a trail that comes out on the road north of Roosevelt Lodge in the north central part of the park. For a while it carries through a forest of fir and softwood. Within a few minutes the sounds of the machine age are swallowed by the rush of the morning wind in the lodgepoles. The breeze fills your nostrils with the scent of resin, so pleasant that you want to put your face to the branches and let its sweet pungence drain into your lungs. In the distance there is a constant and still indefinable rumbling, like a train miles away. It is forgotten for a while, because here is a tubby marmot playing on the boulders off the trail.

Stop one moment.

Consider this plump and vaguely pompous character trundling around the rocks. Try whistling. Some marmots whistle, you have been told. They do, but this one doesn't. This one has a brown coat and yellow belly and a nose as eager as a rabbit's in a cabbage patch. He declines, however, to whistle. What he does is squat on the boulder and stare at you with obvious disapproval. You can retaliate by refusing to share your lunch. You can do that without a seizure of conscience. He may be the fattest marmot you have ever seen, which is a distinction considering the strong competition.

The trail turns north and the rumbling takes on a broader resonance. It will be a cascading stream all right, and it must be a sizable one. The sound has become an insistent boom. Abruptly the trail opens onto a 100-foot suspension bridge. Directly beneath you, brawling and pounding at its rocky encasements, is the River of the Yellowstone itself. The canyon is hundreds of feet deep and yet you swear you can feel the spray on your face. The water is a tumultuous gray-green. It is so swift and violent that you can almost hear it railing against the strictures of those huge walls. There is another impression you can't immediately define.

128

You have seen this river when it was even more powerful and imperial, when its cataracts fell hundreds of feet and hurled themselves through canyons of such depth and beauty the eye seemed inadequate to organize all of the glories at one viewing.

But now you are alone with the river. Leave the bridge for a few minutes and walk the ridge of the bluffs overlooking the river. This is not the Yellowstone of the hot-gusher circuses and the rummaging bears. This is an ocean of grassland and wild forests beyond, and the pounding of the river and the great mountain barriers beyond that. You can lie in the grass and let yourself scan the full 360 degrees of the compass and drift into time, centuries past. Imagine yourself the first human witness to this gigantic canvas of forest, savannah, whitewater and mountain. You could be that witness because you can find no clue or hint that a human has ever been here before.

You are stirred by the harmonies of this limitless nature, and you want to luxuriate in the privacy of it. But mostly you are struck by the pure magnitude of it. This is the mountain west, true and pure, stretching to the edges of one's comprehension.

Let the sunlight and grass tassels frolic on your cheek. The earth smells soft and warm. Open your eyes and track the cumulus ships as they float above you. Let yourself wander again, to meet the images: An Indian hunting party tracking bison; Jim Bridger peering into the mountains for a route, honing the stories he will tell the greenhorns, about fishing in a place so miraculous you could hook a fish in one pool and boil it in another without taking it off the hook.

Time to walk the trail again, toward Hell Roaring Creek, where you can camp for the night. Don't worry about grizzlies. They prefer Hayden Valley, and they never come through here.

Almost never.

Tomorrow you can join the tourists at Norris Geyser Basin. Tonight you will sleep under the lodgepoles and listen to Hell Roaring Creek churning through the boulders and hissing past your tent. There is no one here but you and the river and the forest. You shouldn't have to worry about intruders.

But it isn't a bad idea to hang your food 10 feet off the ground. You might want to make that 20 feet.

VI.
The World Looks Different from a Bicycle Seat

A man and his daughter can bicycle for miles through headwinds and hills without talking. They may grunt appreciatively now and then. But at unpredictable times they will discover something new or funny or deeper about the other, and after that the miles fly by.

A FATHER'S EDUCATION ON WHEELS

In the little rear view mirror on my bicycle's handlebar, I searched for movement behind me near the top of one more hill on the road to the Grand Teton Mountains.

In a moment my daughter's helmet bobbed around a grove of lodgepole pine, and she pumped laboriously up the pebbled asphalt to join me. Sweat bubbles jelled under her eyes, and her helmet was askew. She had to blow some vagrant hair out of her eyes.

"Less than a mile to the top of the pass," I said.

It was a promise, but it may not have impressed Amy. She puffed and swallowed, and put her foot back into the pedal stirrup. The road had risen 5,000 vertical feet since we left Riverton, Wyoming, two days ago, and nearly 9,000 since we left Minneapolis almost 1,200 miles to the east, and none of it was climbed on promises.

We rolled again. The highway dipped insignificantly before the next small brow, but there was something unusual about the behavior of the small creek romping down the slope below it. It was flowing west.

"We've crossed the Continental Divide," I said over my shoulder.

Bobbing and puffing behind me, nothing more.

We stopped. And here beside the road shoulder was a sign. "Togwotee Pass, 9,658 feet."

We had no more mountains to climb or rivers to cross. We hugged. Congratulations, stubborn young lady. She smiled wearily and then scowled. These were the 1980s. To one woman of 21, being described as "a young lady" is an affront, a moldy relic of an old and discredited sexism.

But she smiled again and squeezed me. At 21, the balanced woman of the `80s ought to be mature enough to forgive. We had not reached the Tetons yet. They were still concealed by the intervening ridges. A tourist from Keokuk, Iowa, stopped his house trailer and volunteered to take our picture, and for five minutes we explored the blood lines and histories of the Togwotee travelers, etched on the sign. The westerners call it Toe'-gah-tee. The Crow, Shoshone and Blackfoot Indians crossed here. An Indian guide named Togwotee the Lance Thrower led a white man's expedition through. And this is where the waters divide. To the east they run to the Missouri and Wind rivers, to the west, the Snake and Columbia.

We sat for awhile, each reflecting.

I found myself regretting the approaching end of our small odyssey, for all of the aches and head winds of it. The young woman had been a partner and a companion, and a rather unforgettable one. She had been someone to play road games with and someone to haggle with, and two or three times someone to cry with. But she was also someone to rely on without hesitation.

She had been ailing much of the time. We tried Bromo-Seltzer, Alka-Seltzer and most of the other remedies, plus the maiden aunt's. Still, she pedaled and enjoyed and insisted on veto power over the route we took and the cowboy cafes where we ate. We had battled for days over her contact lenses. She claimed that dust and sweat had been fouling them, so she rode without them, effectively blotting out the prairie monotony en route.

"The object on your left," I said near Lusk, Wyoming, "is a horse. I tell you that because you might have missed it."

This whistling arrow failed to budge her on her bicycle seat.

"I don't have to know the color of his eyes to know it's a horse," she said.

Like any self-respecting expedition, we decided early on a distribution of work. On the road, I performed such acts as cutting the wind, hauling the tent, knocking on farmers' doors for water, carrying the packs and providing the money.

Amy was the navigator and radio operator. She handled the weather reports, made scientific predictions, brought me up to date on her graduation agendas in the ivy parlors at Yale and delivered announcements siphoned from the gossipy little radio stations of the West.

"Brian Atkins and Alice Moore are getting married Saturday near Chamberlain," she disclosed east of Winner, South Dakota.

"Good," I said. "Tell the newlyweds to honeymoon by bicycle. It's a great conditioner for marriage."

She was also the self-designated den mother and etiquette counselor, carefully protecting the family dignity.

"Dad," she said on the Dakota prairie, "I think it would be a good idea for you to change your T-shirt this afternoon."

"The odors of honest labor are nothing to apologize for," I huffed.

"It's just a matter of taste," she said. "Use your own judgment. I just don't want the farmers thinking that you're inconsiderate when you knock for water."

I rummaged in my saddle bags for another shirt when we crossed the mile-long bridge over the Missouri River west of Platte, South Dakota. By then we had adjusted to the voltage of the prairie sun. In 500 miles our skins had acquired a becoming cast of chestnut. We had also acquired the Bedouin's instincts for water conservation and were drinking in trickles instead of gulps. You had to do it. In South Dakota the commercial water supplies

137

may be three hours apart for the bicyclist.

The agronomist sees the Dakota prairie as bountiful and unselfish, a giver of bread and beef for the world's lunchpails and its tables. The bicyclist sees it as that, but he also sees it as the ant probably sees a football field. It seems to have no limits. It seems, in fact, almost invincible in its raw geography. But the mathematics of our ride were pretty rigid. We had to average more than 100 miles a day on our timetable, and if we ran into tornadoes—as we did at Vesta, Minnesota—or 35-mile-an-hour head winds followed by a one-hour hailstorm—as we did near Mitchell, South Dakota—the next day it would be 130 miles.

But it was not an ordeal. We rode the back roads, which meant hours for gabbing or introspection. For me, it also meant discovering a little more each day, in ways surprising, hilarious and sometimes moving, about a young woman I thought I knew so well. I was fascinated by her maturing mind and by some of her intensities. For the first time in our lives we would talk for long periods about the world, it's injustice and its wonders, and our places in it. We talked about her ambitions and her friends. I was pleased to see her compassions and loyalties, and surprised by the level of her anger at the pace of the country's reform to meet the needs of the neglected and abused. But she was fun and sometimes predictable, and she needled the trunks off me.

We had come all these miles together, and we were both older and younger for it. She had been a pixie and a grunt, laboring up hills for an hour at a time without speaking, and then bursting with chatter and plans. She was captivated by the big country, yes. But she been there before, and this time getting there had been the thing. Getting there on the back roads meant the towns were tiny and remote, and we were welcomed in each as visitors from another galaxy. It's not that these people don't watch television and know the world. But the land is their destiny. It is not for larking about the country and experiencing dust on a 15-speed bicycle, but for tilling and harvesting. And the weather for us

138

might have been a conversational mine or a simple inconvenience. For the farmers and ranchers it is often their demon. It is hard for a resident of Aurora Center, South Dakota, therefore, to conceive why anyone would voluntarily bicycle through it for 1,200 miles.

"I don't think you should use the sink water for drinking," a young body and fender man said in Aurora Center. "But I'll be glad to run to my grandma's to fill your bottles."

His grandmother lived nearly a quarter of a mile away. A few hours later when we stopped for information at another farm house, the folks asked us in for lunch and talk. They seemed genuinely sorry when we left. A child in the family gave us a flower, which we preserved, raggedly, for days. It was not hard to blend into this world. South of Stickney, South Dakota, we were adopted by a herd of 30 dairy cows on their way to pasture. For their route, they chose the highway—the full width of it. With no practical choice, we joined them and continued this odd association until one of the cows lifted her tail and splattered the road in front of us with the well-known material. We fell back prudently.

We had ridden in 100-degree heat. We had ridden through the lingering sadness and, yes the guilt, that the comfortable middle class white must experience in the Rosebud Indian Reservation and the land of Wounded Knee. And we had survived an encounter with Hell's Hot Acre.

The rational mind will tell you that Hell's Half Acre, a moon crater unaccountably transported to the high semi-desert in central Wyoming, is only a geological freak. It is not supposed to produce whammies or influence the behavior of bicycles or of people who ride them. But I can only record three events that happened within a few miles of Hell's Half Acre:

I spilled for the first time in a thousand miles, burying my nose in fresh blacktop while the bicycle plowed into a ditch of sagebrush.

My daughter blew her rear tire, again, for the fifth time in six days. She did it imaginatively. She did not run over a broken beer bottle or an abandoned razor blade. She flattened her tire on an office staple. I can't explain how this object came to be lying on the shoulder of one of the loneliest highways in America. But there it was in the prongs of my first aid tweezers when I examined the tube.

The replacement tube in my daughter's rear tire developed a slow leak and had to be reinflated for the next 40 miles in places beyond the reach of surveyors and missionaries alike.

But I pumped the tire, and my daughter struggled to hold some middle ground between looking grateful and laughing out loud.

As I rode, I learned more about my paradoxical young daughter, and I rode with that experience surfacing as the continuing windfall of the trip. Although considerate most of the time, she had no patience for what she called my Ostrich Syndrome as a traveler. Short of the storm forecast, I try to shun so-called trail information volunteered by locals or other trekkers. It's often unreliable, and I prefer discovery. I don't want to know about the length of a hill or the smell of a stagnant pond 15 miles way. There is time enough to find it.

Amy was furious with this attitude and armed herself in advance with all the technology, local prophecies and miscellaneous road chatter. "How can you NOT be prepared?" she demanded, with the autocracy of an Ivy League junior.

The young woman was willful, alert and armed with a 21-year-old's quick and sometimes uncharitable judgment, but also with the resilience. She offered no complaint riding 12 hours in the prairie sun but wailed about the lousy carpentry of an outhouse in Vetal, South Dakota. She was a relentless goal-setter and welcomed hills because they stimulated her adrenalin. But she complained bitterly about getting up in the morning. She knew me much too well to attribute nobility to the good things I do or malice to the bad. While sometimes she crabbed or razzed, she

140

would sometimes see my preoccupation with another part of my life, and there was tenderness in how she edged into my thoughts. She accepted sprains, sunburn and high wind but worried nearly to death about looking ragged riding to town. She was one man's daughter, and the more I thought about it, the less joy I found in the approaching end of the ride.

The rest at Togwotee ended with the onset of storm heads. It was downhill, now, but we did no exuberant leaping from ridge to ridge. The bicycle is a fragile machine. There are powerful mountains. The road dives thousands of feet and forgives no runaways. It was also wet. So we nursed the bicycles mile after mile, surrendering the downhill euphoria to higher demands of self-preservation.

And then the Tetons erupted before us through a clearing in the trees. Did it matter that they have performed that stunning scene of dozens of time. Did it matter that the orchestration of snow and granite were so familiar to us that we could identify every summit, and sense the trail dust in the canyons miles away?

They never lose their spontaneity or mystery, the power to churn the blood. They sweep straight out of the valley in cliffs thousands of feet high, creating peaks stark and virile, competing with each other for the onlooker's wonder.

I first came to the valley of Jackson Hole in the 1950s. The architects and bulldozers have moved the buildings and changed the roads and pulled out most of the commerce, and there is still peace and restoration here. There is excitement if you want it. It is the essence of the national park idea, the ultimate proof that not all of the land must be thrown to the machines to feed the gullet of progress and the gross national product. No gold or uranium is extracted here. Yet it has enlarged the lives of millions of people—whether or not they define it this way. It has turned their directions, permitted them to relocate themselves with nature and to rediscover their earth. You can come to these mountains as hiker, climber, wildflower ogler, as tourist or bicyclist. The Grand

141

Tetons are an ideal, a statement of a wild nature preserved and at the service of the communicant. If you are seeking that ideal, you will usually find.

One last puzzlement overtook my daughter.

"Dad, you must have taken that picture two dozen times over the years."

It wasn't a reprimand. She did wonder if there is any possible new way to take a picture of Mount Moran from the Oxbow Bend of the Snake River. The camera might have agreed, because it was out of film.

"Tommy Tourist strikes out," she mourned.

We had come all that distance, and learned so much. We found deeper worth not only in each other, I think, but in the benevolence of the land we traveled and the people who came into our lives.

We slept well on the shore of Jackson Lake that night, with no more wheels to turn.

The Balkans produce a family album

They biked for a week with alternating joy and bafflement through their ancestral homeland, Slovenia in Yugoslavia, in search of family. For five days they found clues and saw faces that might have been related, but no one knew. This was their sixth and final day.

We located Aloiz today, the one blood relative I'm sure of in the Balkans' ethnic collage.

When we found him, Aloiz was surrounded by his family vineyards in his summer cottage, coasting through three days off from the office and smelling the new geraniums in the window boxes. Right about there, I began to entertain serious questions about my forebears: What was the immigrants' big rush to get to the open pit iron mines of Minnesota 7,000 miles away?

Aloiz Pucelj is full of spring and electricity, a man of movement—impulsive movements and hawkish features. At 48 he bicycles, runs marathons and climbs mountains. He is also the chief of the survey office for Novo Mesto, an industrial city of 50,000. He wore Adidas, jogging pants and a sweatshirt, about all he could find when we walked in on his family through the grapevines.

I apologized and thanked their daughter, Sonja, a law student, for showing the way from town in the taxi. Do you categorize your cab drivers? Try this one. He wore a gray business suit and a floral red tie and sat rigidly behind the wheel, the way Paul Lukas, the old continental actor, might have done it in a spy movie. He was dignified and upright and oblivious of the Balkan sun. He said he could wait as long as we needed, and when we left he turned off the meter for a stroll through the cornfield.

We introduced ourselves to Aloiz and family, and the man started talking in quantum leaps. "I meet my cousins in Minnesota 10 years ago. The only Jeem I have heard of is what you call a troubadour, a teller of stories. Are you that one?"

I said I don't have a mandolin but I probably qualified. He described my mother and said his father and her father were brothers, which made Aloiz and me cousins for sure. We did the embraces, first cooly and then fervently, and graduated from there to kisses on the cheek. Amy joined, and so did Aloiz's wife, Vita, and then Sonja, and in no time it was a De Mille epic.

So life has hardly been an anguish for Aloiz Pucelj. You can pronounce the name with the accent marks in different places, but the Pucelj folks removed the "j" as a reasonable compromise when they got to America.

Aloiz was educated at the university in Slovenia, moved up the surveying echelons and now shuttles with his wife from their large house in Novo Mesto to their new chalet in the country. Most of the farm property belongs to his wife's family, but nobody bothers much with contracts out here in the vineyard.

"What a marvelous life," I said. "The immigrants made a lot of wine in northern Minnesota but the climate wasn't very friendly to grapes, so they often use wild pin cherries from the bush or dandelions."

"Yes, I have tasted these dandelion wine," Aloiz said. As an act of charity, he declined to give an opinion. But I now found him staring at me with much anxiety.

"You people must be starved," he told Marko, our young bicycling interpreter. His alarm sounded genuine. I believe he suspected we were on the verge of collapse.

"It's nine o'clock," Marko said. "We had breakfast an hour ago."

Aloiz wiped away this objection with one run to the wine room and his wife demolished it with a tray from the refrigerator. Each time they stopped at the table the delivery could have accommodated the morning rush at the Lincoln Del.

There was a merciful lull that gave me a chance to measure the voltage levels of hospitality around the world. It's pretty much a universal instinct, but there are variations in how it is pressed on the defenseless guest. I think the Norwegians win one ribbon for the pure acreage of their breakfast spread. But here in the summer home of Aloiz Pucelj it acquired a different tone entirely. This was the first hospitality I've seen that was explosive.

Aloiz came first with glasses of plum brandy. I'm not sure whether these were intended for reserve or for ignition. Without breaking stride he followed with glasses of white wine, red wine, mineral water, tea and coffee. While this movement was on full cycle his wife materialized with platters of pastries, smoked ham and fruit from their orchard.

"Aloiz," I said. "We still have to bike 70 kilometers to Ljubljana."

"But you can't possibly do it on an empty stomach."

He was right. He couldn't possibly escape the platters of ham and pastry. We jabbered nonstop for two hours. After a while I mentioned the cab driver and Aloiz jogged 500 yards to where the car was parked. He said he knew all the cab drivers in Novo Mesto. Ten minutes later he walked in with the cab driver, still wearing his business coat and his red tie and streaming sweat. By now the celebration was general and threatened to spread to the next vineyard. We said we had to leave, but Aloiz wouldn't release us until we promised to stay for two weeks the next time we came.

Nobody escaped the cheek-kissing on the last go-round. Even the cab driver got smacked, and I'm not sure by whom.

We rolled back at leisure to Ljubljana, past the castle in Zuzemberk and through rows of corn 10 feet tall. Because the country has all the components they once wrote fairy tales about, the visitor subconsciously turned the pages. Here were geese in the farmyard, pigs in the barn. Every three miles there was a village and in every village a steeple. There were grapes on the slopes and, beyond them, shaded and mysterious forests. I had expected to find old wooden houses falling down. But from somewhere, the people found enough money to rebuild most of them, and now factory workers commute from comfortable looking stucco houses.

But this was no comic strip Lower Slobbovia. It has witnessed wars, political subjugation and the mass murders by conquerors and their avengers. It has been invaded by Turks, Austrians, Germans, French drivers and American tourists. Yugoslavia shouldn't work and often doesn't. It is a volatile congress of Macedonians, Bosnians, Montenegrans, Serbs, Croats, Slovenes and a half dozen more, tied together more by their old feuds than the bylaws of any federation, whether Communist, socialist or nondescript.

But this was one small interlude in a land of roots for a man and his daughter, riding and walking the land from which people came to America with nothing much more than nametags on their lapels. We found it civil and winsome. Nobody gets paid much here, and the value of the American dollar is indecently out of whack with reality. But you hear a lot of laughing in this country and you see a lot of kissing. I'm not sure how that ranks in the international currency markets, but it makes an unforgettable week.

When we got back to Ljubljana we had to make our goodbyes to Marko. He had been a treasure—courteous, inventive and a man totally immersed in the discovery process himself. Marko

146

said we couldn't possibly get on the train to Austria on an empty stomach. So he hauled us to his apartment. His wife was a show-stopper. She wore jet black hair to her shoulders and might have been a Jean Tierney. She talked affably about music, office work and babies, and I'm sure she was an expert in all three. She also cooked like the chef at Antoine's.

It made two celebrations in eight hours, which is almost two past my limit. Marko took us to the train. More kisses on all appropriate cheeks. It gets to be a habit. There's no telling how I'm going to behave when I get home. I can't remember the last time I offered smoked ham to the Culligan man.

VII.
Shangri-La by Other Names

Except for the novelist, no one has discovered an identifiable Shangri-La, a land of serenity and lotus blossoms. But the Himalayan traveler will come to forests bursting with rhododendrons, listen to the bantering Sherpas and look at snow mountains floating as if in another cosmos. Each upward step is a step backward in time and deeper into the spirit.

What is the difference between reality and the novelist's myth?

A TINY ORCHID AMONG
HIMALAYAN GIANTS

We walked through a forest filled with hanging moss and ancient oaks, sycamore glens and secret moans muted by the wind.

It was the kind of forest that children imagine on their first reading of "Snow White and the Seven Dwarfs." It lay in a fantastic architecture framed by the great snow mountains of the Himalayas and the deepest gorge on earth, the ravine of Kali Gandaki.

But if the Himalayas and the gorge are nature on a scale gigantic, the dark forest was a nature intimate yet mysterious. The uncanny sounds may have been the scraping of the trees, some of them sculpted by age and weather into misshapen figures of torment, oddly dignified. Clearly, the sorcerer had been through here. You could tell by the frightful faces that stared at the intruding travelers from the bark of the old oaks, and by the black rivulet that rippled moodily through the ravine.

But this was not the dominion of the wicked queen. Annapurna ruled here.

Annapurna is the Nepalese goddess of giving, the protector of the harvest. And because Annapurna the mountain lifted its veils of ice 20,000 feet above us, why should it be a surprise to find ourselves walking among wild orchids during a snowfall?

Nothing can surprise the trekker in this mind-stretching land of white spires, yak trains, holy men, villages a thousand years old and rhododendron forests.

On the first night of our trek through the Kali Gandaki a hailstorm rattled our tents and thunderbolts stoked up a bedlam across the ice fields three miles above us.

On the second day we walked through forests of bamboo and banana trees under a tropical sun, and on the third we slogged over a pass at 9,500 feet in a snowstorm and caught slush in the face from a passing yak. To escape a cloudburst on the fourth day we took sanctuary for the night in a smoky Nepalese inn inhabited by one family, three chickens and a small pig. And by the sixth day we were bending into a 40-mile-an-hour dust storm hurtling across the desert.

Is this the legendary Shangri-La?

Let me offer a proposition. It is better if you find it a tantalizing thought to be part of a tiny caravan of middle-agers from Minnesota, four women and two men, moving through a time warp in which waterfalls, caverns, glaciers, vast mountains and the faces and tongues of Asia compete for the travelers' amazement.

This is not the never-never land of the fictitious Shangri-La, with its fountain mists escorting the pilgrim through arbors of lotuses. There are no kids in sack clothes and runny noses begging for sweets in Shangri-La, no foot blisters or sand in the teeth.

You will find those things on a trek through the Kali Gandaki. But there are also files of ponies, announced by their melodic bells and scarlet plumes, threading the trails of one of the world's oldest trade routes. There are Tibetan herdsmen in black fur helmets, holy men on their way to the mountain shrine of Muktinath; there are squawking chickens and chanting old men. Suspension bridges pitch the traveler into the comic gyrations re-membered from carnival rides, and mossy woods erupt into blossoms of rhododendrons and orchids.

And there is Ang Nima ahead of us, walking through those dark woods and blossom thickets. I'm no horticulturist—I didn't know they were orchids. Ang called them that. If there were something supernatural in this forest, then Ang was one of its solemn elves, a brown little man with a face and hands roughened by the Himalayan gales and years of grunt work as a climbing Sherpa porter. Near a stream Ang left the trail and we stopped while he silently explored one of its low-hanging limbs. He lifted his arms and plucked one of the orchids, held it between his thumb and forefinger with great tenderness and extended it to us, as though sharing a treasure of his house.

This was a man who walked for miles with frostbite through eight feet of fresh snow, wearing camp stools for snowshoes. He went to sound the alarm for a team of trekkers marooned without food in the Tilicho Pass three years before. Four Sherpas on the team lost their lives in a snowslide trying to push a rescue attempt to the other side of the pass.

Although there are a few hustlers and hard drinkers among them, most of the Sherpas are like Ang, capable of great sacrifice and rather heroic acts. Yet the Sherpas are still willing—by in-stinct —to perform the most menial work in a robust and totally gleeful way. It is a part of their Buddhism and it is a quality that can turn a trek from drudgery to frolic.

Trekking in the Himalayan style, in which porters carry and Sherpas do the housekeeping and humor the laggards, does not demand super creatures or valiant behavior. Older folks do it more than younger ones, primarily because you need some age to accumulate the $2,500 to $3,500 in air fare and ground costs for the standard trek. You have to come with liberal attitudes toward dirt coagulating in the more awkward seams of your body, toward the co-ed use of the camp latrine tent and to fatigue. There are days

153

when you will gain 3,000 feet on trails that were built a thousand years ago, well before tourism was seriously contemplated in the Himalayas. But for people in average physical condition, it is well within range. Inevitably, the image of the Himalayas as a land of a spiritual epiphany will stir in the mind of the trekker, particularly in those heady weeks of preparation.

It is not totally misplaced. Although Nepal is a land of smothering poverty, the visitor—particularly the second- and third-time visitor—will feel a spiritual magnetism among the monasteries and in the faces of the devout. It is not easily defined. It is not necessarily intensely felt. But it is there, and it can be humbling.

The idea of a Shangri-La, the longing for an experience that will somehow bring a transfiguring peace and wisdom to the traveler, is lovely and poetic. But it has wrecked more Himalayan treks than bad food and lousy weather. If there is no Santa Claus or red-nosed reindeer, there also is no place where the enigmas of creation and the grumps of daily living are going to be explained in one sunburst of revelation. If you come to the Himalayas, though, do it with a serviceable set of lungs, durable feet and an open mind. You may not be transfigured but you may very likely be amazed. You may also emerge with a revised picture of yourself, and you certainly will emerge wiser.

I can affirm the truth of this maxim.

My most indispensable role in the troupe was to act daily as the route-finder to the homely blue tent, the necessary room. In fairness I have to say this role came to me more because of my familiarity with climbing techniques than to any superior claim to the blue tent's services. The Sherpas normally try to locate it in a place that meets minimum standards of convenience and privacy. But at Chandrakot, we were camped on the edge of a small cliff. Convenience would have subjected the user to a nosedive of 100 feet if he or she emerged with the left foot instead of the right. So the blue tent was installed on a terrace 15 feet above the campsite. This offered privacy. Unhappily, one of the two approach routes took the user straight through a water buffalo compound. The route we adopted was less hazardous but more strenuous. It meant the client had to step over four guy ropes of the dining tent, thread through a steep and narrow brick water chute for 20 feet and then vault a wire fence three feet high before gaining the outer flap of the blue tent.

I was assigned the first night patrol. By using advanced principles of leverage, I cleared the guy wires and did a straight frontal assault on the water chute. Impelled by the normal urgencies, I jumped the three-foot fence and was prepared to raise a victory flag when the rays of my flashlight found an alien object near the tent flap. It looked like a horn. When I looked again, I saw a second horn. That made sense, because both horns belonged to a head, and the head was attached to the biggest water buffalo I ever saw. I can only say that my urgency ended on the spot.

If I emerged wiser from the Himalayas each visit, I'm mortally certain that Jackie Neubauer emerged with new concepts of The Organized Woman.

By the time we reached the Gandaki River and its plum orchards, its sandstorms and its stupendous geography—Annapurna and Dhaulagiri rising five miles above the valley—Jackie already had created a sensation on the trail. She is tall and athletic, 48, a resident of St. Bonifacius, Minnesota, and a relatively recent convert to the outdoor cult. Although restrained in most of her habits and stubbornly unshowy, she had acquired a pair of tomato red, full length tights as part of her biking regalia. She brought them to the Himalayas for the cool mornings and wore them daily until the sun forced the usual 10:00 A.M. peeling exercises. The sight of this striking figure in her flaming pants stopped most traffic for two weeks in a part of the world where other phenomena, such as avalanches, rarely draw a second glance. In the town of Dana the villagers were disappointed when she showed up in basic walking shorts. The Kali Gandaki bamboo telegraph was that conscientious.

155

This aside, Jackie quickly acquired notoriety in our troupe as a remorseless pack rat. She arrived with a vast arsenal of bottles, jars, vats and tubes, dedicated to keeping Jackie Neubauer free of all known mountain diseases and growths. Each of these she labeled and stashed in a pre-arranged niche in her duffel bag every morning.

Unfortunately she was victimized daily by her organizational zeals. By noon she could never remember which remedy was stashed where. Her film met the same fate.

"I can't take a picture," she wailed through the Gandaki riverbed's blowing sand. "I thought I wrapped my unused film in my undies and my used film in a dirty sock. It must have been the other way. I grabbed the wrong film from the duffel bag, and the duffel bag is with the porters 10 miles away." What she produced from her pack was a pair of undies and a roll of used film. Neither seemed especially useful in the Kali Gandaki windstorm.

In time, Jackie was reunited with her film. And in time, Sonam Chottem, the young Sherpa who was the sirdar of our trek, was reunited with the eternal blue flame.

The blue flame burns underground in a small pit guarded round-the-clock by one of the penitents in the monastery at Muktinath. There, Buddhists and Hindus alike cleanse their bodies and souls by washing in the water of 108 fountains created by streams flowing from the perpetual snows.

Is that a fairy tale?

I didn't smile when Sonam related it. The hill people have to exercise some restraint themselves not to smile when they are told how another god could arrive 4,000 miles away by being born to a virgin.

So the Buddhist Sherpa and Christian trekker walked together to the holy flame. We gained altitude quickly by moonlight, through the tight desert canyon, past the towns of Marpha and Jomson. To the north spread the plateau of Tibet, the only place on earth where the desert and arctic geographies merge. We stood at

daybreak in an amphitheater of silence, immense and unfathom-
able. Alpenglow lit the snow summits above us and crept down
toward the stands of Himalayan fir and juniper beneath the
snowline. Farther south along the river, groves of plums, oranges
and bananas softened the red sandstone walls of the canyon
through which the dark river flowed. Nothing could have changed
much here from the time of Marco Polo, Gautama Buddha or Jesus
Christ. The acoustics of the place were startling. From distant
miles you could hear the chimes from the bells of a Tibetan pony
carrying a solitary traveler. He passed us wearing blankets and a
high-crowned black fur cap. His face was grave and mahogany,
weary and ageless. We exchanged greetings, and he disappeared
into the dust of time.

We hiked above the terraced slopes of potato and buckwheat
farms tilled by men driving water buffalo, their wives casting seed
behind them. On a promontory below the shrine were the ruins of
a castle, where 1,500 years ago a king ruled. What kind of king? A
cruel king. It's written. There are very few fairy tales in the
Himalayas. Most of it has happened.

I don't know if those waters Sonam bathed in from the 108
fountains are blessed. Why shouldn't they be? The flame burned
from natural gas, but natural gas is a wonder of its own. Muktinath was holy to Sonam because he believes in the sacredness of
his mountains. His eyes told it a few days before when we saw
Machupuchare, the mountain shaped like an elegant fish's tail.
The Nepalese believe it is blessed, and it may be, because there are
few mountains in the world lovelier. It rose into the sunset like a
chalice, lifted by unseen arms above a vestment of clouds.

And when we left Muktinath, Sonam shook my hand sol-
emnly and pronounced the word of greeting that is traditional in
these mountains:

Namaste. I hail the god that lives within you.

A walk in the Himalayas is worthwhile simply knowing there
is such a thought.

THE SAINT WITH A DUSTY GOWN
AND SORE FEET

An incense stick burned in the ash tray of my taxicab. The smoke curled around the driver's shoulders and pressed against my face like scented angel hair. From the dashboard, the symbols of the driver's gods stared at me speculatively.

Nothing should astonish you about the streets of Katmandu.

It would have been a transporting moment in the cab except that the machine was charging through the streets oblivious of all rules of gravity and simple chance.

We ducked sacred cows, beggars, rickshaws, chickens and terrified pedestrians. What we couldn't duck we intimidated with the horn and squealing brakes. I say "we" because I was totally dependent on the driver for the rankest level of survival. What I was doing, to be honest, was hanging on and looking for a soft curb. The destination didn't matter by then. For most cab drivers in Katmandu, style and suspense outrank the bland moments of safe delivery.

When we got there, the driver turned and smiled benevolently. He took my sweat-smeared rupees and, bowing slightly, joined his palms and fingertips in the Nepalese gesture of greeting and thanks. It always disarms me. There is a lyricism in this part of the world that outreaches the poverties and stenches, the

159

overpopulation and sickness. It also seems to make sense out of the clang and tumult of the streets, and it gives tone to the luminous morning above the Himalayas' blue ice fields.

Here there is a tolerance of time and destiny that would not be accepted where we live in the West, partly because of how we live. We live with comfort and supercharged urgency. Goals and deadlines. Net worth, quality time, rollovers—and make sure it's all in your will because you may have a coronary.

We also spend billions of dollars trying to figure out why all of that hasn't produced harmony in our lives.

We spend it for therapy, counseling, treatment, reinforcement, potions for health, pathways to greatness and antidotes for burnouts.

It's barely possible that in this pell-mell quest for peace of mind we have overlooked an older and more durable wisdom— a wisdom that can be found beneath the snows of the Himalayas.

I went to the Himalayas this time not only as a trekker but also as a man with questions, and with open eyes and ears. You can set aside the shaggy-dog sagas about the meaning of life and the dreams of Shangri-La. No identifiable Shangri-La has yet been discovered in the Himalayas, no Abominable Snowman, and the last Eastern wise man who claimed to know the meaning of life was deported from the United States, and it cost him a fortune.

But to watch the pilgrimage of the devout to the shrine in the sky in Muktinath in the Annapurna range, from valley peasants to the holy men from India hundreds of miles away, is instructive and humbling. Most of these people are ragged and many of them are barefoot. Their eyes bespeak a mingling of hope and resignation. There are Hindus and Buddhists, occupied with a stable of deities and rituals that befuddle the Westerner. But their poverty does not disable them psychologically or spiritually. They seem to wear dirt and discomfort with equal acceptance. These are not high priests, the interpreters of Vishnu and Siva, but the dirt-floor believers, the ones who might have more to teach the inquisitive

160

One of the Andes' highest, Huascaran, at 22,000 feet, floats two miles above a Peruvian village not far from the equator.

The tiny women of the Peruvian foothills live a spare and difficult life, but for a wedding they dress in their rainbow best.

Their faces smeared with zinc oxide for protection, Rod Wilson, Doug Kelley and Peruvian Fausto Cleva ready for Huascaran.

Sunlight burnishes the glacia ice as climbers thread throug crevasses on Huascaran.

The tropical sun ignites the Andean heights and turns th slopes of Huascaran into a furnace for the climbers.

A nearby basin of hot springs flocks the pines and creates a forest of fantasy.

Skiers skim through fresh snow along Nez Perce Creek in the heart of Yellowstone.

Nourished by the geysers, a stream offers its delicate colors and warmth to an uncanny montage of Yellowstone.

The paradox of Yellowstone
in winter: cauldrons among
the icefields.

A river gives character to the
downtown of Lubljana in
Yugoslavia.

If you search for distant kin in
Slovenia, you have to hug a
lot of people.

A tiny shrine shelters a wood carving on the road from Austria to Lubljana in Slovenia.

A day on the road ends in a squeeze. Jim and daughter Amy, partners on one more biking odyssey.

Rhododendrons create a
graceful arbor below the
Himalayas' citadels of ice.

She offers bells, bracelets and a social bout of bargaining to the Himalayan trekker.

On the high road to Nepal, a tradesman smiles a greeting.

Waiting for a load near the airstrip at Lukla on the way to Namche Bazaar.

Village kids laugh at those strange garments of the people who came tenting.

A peak lances the sky near
Everest, almost perfect in it
symmetry.

An avalanche flings its
treacherous white cloud down
a Himalayan slope.

When you walk the bridges of
the Himalayas, you keep your
eyes off the river and your
feet out of the cracks.

The Tetons define the
mountainous West for
millions of travelers and
clans of hikers.

Unaware of an approaching
blizzard, snowmobilers tend a
disabled machine in the
Beartooth.

Glenn Exum's last climb on
the Grand Teton was a carol
to a good life.

Westerner. Here at an ancient crossroads in a wild and arid ravine beneath Annapurna and Dhaulagiri I met five swamis from India, some of them turbaned and cloaked, and all of them hungry.

They were walking the road to Muktinath, on the trail Marco Polo followed a half millennium ago. The inn was scruffy and basted with smoke, but it offered the only nourishment and shelter from the beating Himalayan sun for miles in any direction. The one who spoke English identified himself as Swami Kesova Moni of Agra, India. He walked with a dirty brown gown, an air of fraternal good will and the sore feet of a man who had been on the road for 18 days. The Westerner who makes only sporadic visits to Asia has trouble sorting through the layers of monks, gurus, priests and miscellaneous wise men. Many deserve veneration. Others are hustlers. Some have devoted themselves to decades of contemplative life and have found a discipline and tranquility that seem close to supernatural. They carry the title of master, or teacher, and can do things physically that in anyone else would be called magical.

I asked Swami Moni who he is.

"I am a saint," he said forthrightly.

I found this impressive. I had never before met a self-designated saint. What he meant by sainthood, he explained, was the pursuit of a life of austerity. What he did was study and serve people.

"What does a saint do?" I asked.

"I meditate. I have no material possessions, but I am at peace with myself. I don't mean to say I sit in a corner and think. I am part of the world. Being part of the world means feeling the hardship of a pilgrimage to Muktinath, to be blessed by the waters from its sacred fountains. But it is remarkable what one can do by letting the body and mind work as one, to concentrate, removing from the mind all of the poisons, the anger and resentments."

And is there something special in the Himalayas, a spirit that enhances the search?

177

"There is. Here in these highest mountains there is no turmoil of the city, no warring politics between countries, or the meanness we see. People who live here and come here, of course, have the common human faults. But these high places are the center of powerful religious currents. You can feel them. You can come out of these mountains cleaner in soul."

But why can't that be done by someone living in New York or Minnesota?

"It can. But it's harder because you have so many things to distract you. I came to this feeling only after learning about myself and renouncing all material things, mainly money, belongings and sex."

It occurred to me that the saint might have a hard time recruiting in Minneapolis. But what he said deserved thought. If it deserved emulation, then you would have to make some very serious decisions.

He asked if I could buy his lunch of rice, lentil sauce, chapatis and tea. I said I would be glad to.

"Can you also buy lunch for my four friends?"

I did. I don't know if I felt cleansed. But I did feel lighter.

The swami was a help. I would find more in the days ahead. If you see a path to enlightenment through discipline, renunciation and self-control, you'd better give it some time and humility. There is such a path. It doesn't have to be in the Himalayas. There are variations of that path, not as severe, but as important. The swami didn't blush to ask me to pay for the food. I suppose you could call that a fee for insights of value. The swami would have called it service.

I like that better.

VIII.
The Mixed Moments of Tears and Song

The mountains are places of division and harmony, yearning, death and new beginning. That is true anywhere else on earth. But in the high world, it seems written larger.

A MAN SINGS A FAREWELL
TO HIS MOUNTAIN

Mountains can't sing. It's a truth of nature that wrings no dispute from geologists with their little steel hammers or voice coaches with their metronomes.

Mountains can make echoes and they can thunder with avalanches and roar with rockfall. But they are made of granite and snow and frozen lava. So how could a mountain harmonize with this 70-year-old man who was moving on its skyline, smiling and humming in the breeze and letting the gusts romp in his hair?

The mountain couldn't sing, but it did harmonize. The old man and the mountain, the Grand Teton of Wyoming, were a duet. They had been for 50 years, exactly 50 years, which is why Glenn Exum was singing as he climbed, although he had two cancer operations the last two years. Yet the song spoke not of a requiem but an anniversary.

Some of his friends called it Glenn Exum's last climb on the Grand, on the route he pioneered a half century before to this very day. He was a college kid in the early 1930s, wearing a pair of borrowed football shoes and carrying a length of clothesline. He climbed it alone, this steep salmon-colored rock ridge that has become the most popular rock climb in America. In time they gave the ridge his name, and he became the mountaineer-in-residence in the Grand Teton National Park. As the chief of the climbing school and guide service, he had introduced the climbing ethic to thousands of people. Technique, he said, was important. Strength? It was helpful but not always necessary. Humility? That was critical. Know what you can do, what you can't, learn about

weather and equipment, how to control your body, the resilience
of the body. But above all, learn to respect a day in the mountain
for what it could do for your mind and heart as well as your body.

People came in increasing numbers to the mountains as
climbing became an acceptable recreation in American outdoor
life. Some came to be thrilled or to be indoctrinated, but Exum did
neither. He was a mountain man, but also a man of music. He
taught music in a high school in Idaho and instinctively he viewed
the world as a place for rhythm and harmony. He shunned
theatric postures and hungers of the ego that so often drive
climbers higher and farther, faster and more desperately.

He understood a lot of those urges. He had a few himself. But
although he climbed the Grand Teton more than 300 times, and
although others who climbed the mightiest snow peaks in Asia
marveled at his velvet movements on a mountain, climbing was
not the fuel of his life.

His wife, Beth, mattered much more. His family and friends
did. Harmony did.

Climbing a summit, he said, didn't heighten a person's worth
or put him or her in a clan of the select. He told the novices who
came: Accept a climb for what it is, a rare walk into the heights,
and for what it can tell you. It can tell you about strength you
weren't aware of and satisfactions you didn't think you could
achieve. It might tell you something about adversity and dealing
with defeat, if you want to call it that. It can teach you that in order
to deserve a height, you have to exert and to test your limits.

He was professorial, but he was droll and he was even roguish
in his campfire stories among his friends. Style was important to
Glenn. Harmony. He was tidy and precise, in tending his wisp of
a mustache, in how he wore his climbing clothes and cared for his
equipment and how he glided on the rock. In his youth he was a
man of remarkable good looks and he might have been a movie
star. A producer offered him a screen test in the 1930s. He said no,
teaching music and climbing was what he did. To those of us on

his anniversary climb, he seemed to have mastered the values of the good and productive life, more so than almost anyone we had met. He was a thoughtful husband and father and a craftsman on a mountain or in the concert hall. He seemed incapable of speaking badly of another human. He approached his mountains that way. They give you, he said, in accordance with you bring. If you bring a generous spirit, you will probably come away fulfilled. If you bring a competitive spirit, be careful. The mountains are not things to compete with. Nor did he. Which is why any day on a mountain, in rain, starlight or in sun, was a day of music and order for Glenn Exum.

That is how it was on his 50th anniversary on the mountain. His companions on the ropes were professional climbers who had worked with him for years, amateur climbers who enjoyed both the mountain and Glenn's company, two or three international climbing stars and a neighbor or two from the sagebrush valley beneath the Tetons.

Three months before, he could not have done it. Cancer and the surgery weakened him. The operation succeeded. But it was impossible for him to walk for weeks until not long before the climb. The climb mattered because there was something very symmetrical and right about making a 50th anniversary climb with friends.

And when he got onto that high salmon ridge, the decades peeled away and the pain receded. He climbed and climbed. He was first on the rope while the younger men gaped. Impulsively, near the top, after one delicate step, we all applauded him. We could hear him singing, and the harmony came from the wind and the congeniality of the hour. When we got to the summit, somebody patched a telephone call to the valley. He said to his wife, "Darling, we're here at the top." We. Not I.

There are thousands of climbers. There are not many mountaineers.

This was one of the few.

185

A FROLIC IN THE SNOW ENDS IN GRIEF

Hugh died a few hundred feet beneath the snow crown of the Beartooth Pass.

He died from the effects of cold and fatigue on what was intended to be a weekend frolic in the snow by a group of 14 men, a woman and a teenage boy. His death could have been avoided. We could have limited the number in the snowmobile party. We could have anticipated the blizzard. We could have brought tents and sleeping bags. We could have stayed home.

That is hindsight. It deserves to be made. I don't know if Hugh would have looked at the death of another man, as useful and civilized as he was, and called it purposeless under the same conditions. It could be described that way.

I think he would have been tolerant if curious. He had both qualities in abundance. He had others as strong. The quality he did not have the night of that screaming winter wind was good luck.

The rest of us did.

Even at a distance of two decades, it hurts to examine the might-have-beens of Hugh Galusha's death. They are still tormenting. They are personal. When an experience in the wild country comes to grief it can be derided as foolish or pointless, especially if undertaken purely for fun or recreation. If, on the other hand, you go to the wilderness or the high country and come back without mishap, or even if you come back with no real gratification, you can always find something redeeming in it. It was good for the spirit, good for the health, good for the family. Something was discovered. But when a man dies on what was meant to be a carefree romp in the snow, there are no compensations that matter.

All of which leaves a question: Does that necessarily make the idea, the trip itself, a folly?

All you can say for certain is that it went wrong, and a man of great worth died.

I spoke in these terms to his surviving family members, in a way that perhaps Hugh himself would have tried to explain it. They were generous and listened. They could not possibly have been convinced, although they knew he looked forward to the weekend.

The prospect of racing over the Beartooth in winter intrigued him, as a man who had devoted much of his life to the enhancement of Yellowstone. It was a part of the West, not far where he grew up in Montana, a part of the earth that was important to his family.

No highway route in the American West is more spectacular than the road over the Beartooth Pass of Wyoming and Montana northeast of Yellowstone. From the east it rises from the tourist and mining town of Red Lodge, Montana, to alpine forests, granite walls and cascades, peaking at nearly 11,000 feet.

From the summit it spirals and glides for miles to the entrance of Yellowstone, preparing the tourist for sensations that may be more renowned but no more memorable than the ones the Beartooth has produced.

That is the Beartooth of summer. Until the 1960s, nobody seriously considered a trip over the Beartooth Pass in winter.

In winter the gales and snowstorms can smother visibility in the Beartooth Mountains, and temperatures dive to arctic depths. The road is closed to all wheeled traffic and left to the drifts. A few skiers and snowshoers had experienced it in winter, but mostly as hunters and wardens, almost never in pure curiosity. But the creation of the snowmobile, a machine that skims the snow on a lugged belt, opened parts of America once all but inaccessible in winter to recreationists. That country included the northwoods, the mountains, and roads like the Beartooth Highway.

Two sides to the dispute arose about the propriety of the snowmobile. On the one hand, shouldn't the natural preserves and the high country be spared mechanized intrusion in places once ruled by silence? And on the other, why shouldn't the citizen who is stirred by high country be allowed to see and feel it if the means are available to do it, and to do it with respect for the country?

Arguments could be made on both sides.

In the winter of 1971 we went to the Beartooth with snowmobiles.

Some of us had been there before on machines in winter. A game warden of the territory, Vern Waples, was on the trip, partly as a guide and partly because he enjoyed running the snow of the high country. His wife, self-sufficient and gregarious, was the only woman on the trip. The others filled the spectrum of occupations and outdoor experience: Vern Hennessy, an assistant superintendent of Yellowstone; Monte Later, an Idaho businessman and outdoorsman; Elmer Rucker, an Idaho youth counselor and wilderness trekker; Jim Marshall and Paul Dickson, Minnesota Vikings football players; two professional photographers; two snowmobile mechanics; Bob Leiviska, a Minneapolis insurance man and his teenage son; Wally Dayton, a Minneapolis conservationist and businessman; and Hugh Galusha, the president of the Ninth Federal Reserve Bank in Minneapolis and a conservationist. Some of them were longtime friends of mine. I brought them together at Red Lodge and arranged for a mid-trip overnight stay in a tourist store and lodge called Top of the World, seven or eight miles beyond the summit zone of the highway. It was closed for the winter but we had permission to use it if needed.

Under normal conditions, the snowmobile ride from an over-look some 2,500 feet below the summit to Cooke City can be negotiated comfortably in a day. We allowed for two. Our party wasn't intended to number 16. Two or three of the original group invited friends. We had a relaxed attitude about that. This wasn't an expedition to the headwaters of the Yukon. It was a ride. The walk-ons didn't have to provide documents of admission. They were competent to travel with us and they were welcomed as friends.

But the party was larger than it should have been, which was an important element in the erosion of time as we moved up the mountain.

The snow machines of those years lacked some of the refine-ments of today's. When the mechanical breakdowns came, some of them the result of the thinner altitude, they disrupted our timetables early. The blizzard wrecked them later. If a machine needed servicing, we all stopped. We stopped partly to help and partly to socialize. It was one of those typical snow safaris, chummy and low-pressure.

But by late afternoon the wind had risen from a breeze to a high altitude gale, and as the sun lowered to the horizon, we were riding in a winter hurricane.

The machines began to cut out. When they did, we shared the remaining snowmobiles that were serviceable. Hugh and I rode together for several miles. He was droll and unworried, joshing about the weather and his dubious choices for companions on a Saturday night. He seemed altogether content to absorb the sensations of being two miles high in the mountains in the midst of winter. The gigantic landscape of rock and snow and stands of fir, so familiar to him as a Montanan, now revealed a special mood and texture that oddly conveyed an intimacy with its power. For

190

a few brief hours it was ours and ours alone. The delays caused him no concern. We pretended to hold serious, Pentagon-style conferences about alternative Plans B, C and Z. But because of the malfunctions and the weather, the party began unavoidably to split by late afternoon. Some were walking. As our machine began to lose power, I offered it to Hugh. He said he wouldn't have the faintest idea how to deal with the beast if it had to be humored. He joined Monte Later and Bob Leiviska on foot and waved as he disappeared into the slanting snow.

With the arriving night, it was clear that most of us were not going to reach the Top of the World shelter for the night. And none did.

Five of us, the last of the 16 to reach the summit at nightfall, lay together in the white hurricane, our arms and legs wrapped about each other to share the dwindling warmth in our bodies. Beyond our heavy snowmobile suits, there was nothing to cover us. Not even the snow clung. The night wind, driving the snow before it at speeds from 60 to 90 miles an hour, seemed full of vengeance and derangement, as though we had offended its keepers by coming so high. Wally Dayton, Elmer Rucker, Dave Boe, Vern Hennessy and I packed into a small depression beneath a rock formation. It cut some of the storm's strength but deepened our estrangement from the living world. Near us the snowmobiles squatted in the snow. One or two were operable, but it was impossible to see more than a few feet through the stinging sleet, and somewhere in the impenetrable night the mountain walls fell thousands of feet.

Once every hour or so we would get up to run in place. We talked little, even after the wind slowed and it was evident that we would survive the night. The temperature, mercifully, held at moderate levels. Subzero cold in that wind would have killed us. What little conversation we had focused on the others. Where were they, and were they safe?

Vern Waples had advanced beyond the rest of us before his

machine went out. He walked miles before reaching the floor of a high valley. There he dug a snowcave near the frozen shore of Long Lake, cut some boughs and made a bed for himself. Averil Kronick, a photographer, and Loren Miller, one of the snowmobile mechanics, walked all night in the diminishing wind toward Top of the World. Jim Marshall, Paul Dickson, Dee Street, the other mechanic, Marilyn Waples and Bobby Leiviska, the boy, fought their way through the blizzard and chest-high drifts by picking out a line along the 20-foot poles that served as winter road markers. Marilyn passed within a few feet of where her husband slept safely in his snow cave, unaware that he was near or safe. When they got to a sheltered part of the big forest near the lake, Jim Marshall burned some checks to light a fire, and they, too, were safe.

That made 13 of us at some stage of security as the blizzard played out and gave way to the approaching dawn. Monte Later and Bob Leiviska had battled for hours to achieve some shelter for themselves and Hugh in a three-foot trench dug into the mountain slope a thousand feet from where the five of us slept. They tried covering it with plastic tarp. The gales defeated them. The trench gave the illusion of protection, but the winds pounded them for hours and slowly reduced Hugh's last reserves. He was tired from the trudge from the summit and tired from a demanding business schedule. He sat in the corner of the trench as the night deepened, visited frequently by the others. He slept but responded when the others asked how he felt, and made no complaint. He said each time, "I'm all right." He was a man of buoyancy, mental agility, very much a man of the world, a man of family and a man of great sociability. What came, he could handle. He made no alibis.

He could not have known he was dying. He would have spoken and asked for help. When it was too late, they realized the extremity of his condition. His hands were hardening. They tried frantically to warm him, to bring him back. They breathed into his mouth. There was still life. They stayed with him, rubbing his hands and face, breathing into him.

He died a half hour before the five of us came down from the top to join them.

We were too shattered to cry. We cried the next day when we returned to take Hugh from the mountain.

Twenty years later, I still cry remembering the night bedlam and the quiet death of Hugh.

AUTUMN GIVES WAY GRACEFULLY ON THE TRAIL

A boy, Gerald, nine, wrote to say he was troubled by the shrinking space left to the true adventurer. He said he would like to reach the poles and cross deserts and climb mountains, but most of it had been done.

No doubt, that is a crisis.

He asked whether there was something far away and big that he could circle on a map and train for, so that some day he would know what Hillary and Tenzing felt the day they reached the summit of Mt. Everest.

I replied to Gerald. I told him not all the mountains had been climbed. Not all the horizons reached. But there would be enough of those for his inquisitive mind and restless feet in the years ahead. I offered an invitation to a nine-year-old boy:

You should not try to measure your reward with a scale of miles you have come or altitude you have reached, or value those hours by the number of people who recognize your name.

You can find another prize, and there is almost no way to place a value on it. And that is discovering what the earth has brought into your life. While you are doing it you will experience certain moments when you and the earth are united, when you feel you are indivisible from the wind and the rock and you share their strength, but also the rules of the universe that govern them. That moment will not be a time for feeling awed or humbled or inconspicuous, but for understanding that however we, or you, define God, there is something divine in that moment.

You don't have to be alone to experience it, but perhaps you will be.

There is a place in the Grand Teton mountains called the Cascade Canyon trail. It lifts you out of the historic valley called Jackson Hole and lets you walk among the spires. For three miles it carries you beside the jade stream, which sometimes swishes thoughtfully and sometimes roils and charges. Later, the trail vaults beyond the glacial canyons and avalanche chutes, past a tiny lake called Solitude and scales the steep slope of granite and scree to a flat tundra. It is a barren place of glacial gravel, dwarf pine and struggling alpine flowers, Paintbrush Divide. It is the kind of goal we can manage today on one last hike of the fall.

On another day we can climb the mountains, when we have our equipment and time. But one does not have to reach the summit to deserve the special grace of this place.

So we will hike it together, walking in the mountains among the Douglas fir and beside the swishing stream. We need no conquests today, and no gravity-defying deeds. This will be a small requiem for the season for us on the trail.

It has not rained for days and our boots create puffs of trail dust. After a while the dust lightly powders our face as though it were a cosmetic of the hills. The wind is rising quickly. Thousands of feet above us it creates a phenomenon. A zinc-colored cloud has rolled in from the west but the sun above it shines undiminished. The wind is blowing so hard across the eastern slope of the range that it is shattering the clouds as soon as they touch the violent cross-currents. Is this a game or a war between those mighty forces of our universe, the sun and wind and the invisible powers of the sky? Whatever it is, it's a remarkable sight.

Here in the firs there is shelter from the fallout of those

196

collisions. There can't be many humans in these mountains today, so it is also our hermitage. On this trail, at this moment, there is nothing but the stream, the forest, the mottled walls, the wind, and us.

You are held by a feeling of possessiveness. It's not a greedy feeling. It's light and secretive. Hundreds of thousands of people have roamed these mountains for months. But they are gone now to their drawing boards, shops and television parlors. There are no sounds here but the wind and the stream's. At the top of the divide, the wind breaks full. It is a gale, stinging your face. It tears open the lips and flings cold draughts inside of you. You want to shout back a salutation and a farewell. The fall is giving up its stewardship in the mountains to the winter and the north wind.

On the way down, it begins. The first snowflakes fall, wet and sloppy. We are not impatient, but winter is. And I hear my own words to Gerald echo in my ears: You can find another prize, and there is almost no way to place a value on it.

PHOTO ACKNOWLEDGMENTS

Most of the photos in this book were taken by Rod Wilson. The two of Spitsbergen in the sun are the work of Hertha Grondal, who was then living in Austria. Photos of the giraffes and lions in Africa are by Kjell Bergh. The photos of Ensign Lake, Palisade Head, the canoeist and the Temperance River in northern Minnesota were taken by Rod Wilson's late and beloved brother, Robert Ashley Wilson. The photo of Jim and Amy is courtesy of Duffer Schultz; that of Jim in Yellowstone is by Doug Kelley. The photo of Rod Wilson on the Matterhorn summit, that of Rod, Doug Kelley and Fausto Cleva in the Andes and several of the photos in Africa and Yugoslavia are by Jim Klobuchar.